FILM PROGRAMMING FOR PUBLIC LIBRARIES

ALA Editions purchases fund advocacy, awareness, and accreditation programs for library professionals worldwide.

Public Library Association
a division of the American Library Association

FILM PROGRAMMING FOR PUBLIC LIBRARIES

Kati Irons

ala
editions

An imprint of the American Library Association
Chicago | 2014

Kati Irons is currently the audiovisual collection development librarian for the Pierce County Library System, Tacoma, Washington. She selects and maintains a 500,000-item audiovisual collection for the eighteen-branch system, which serves 560,000 people, and manages an AV budget that has increased from $30,000 in 1991 to more than $700,000 in 2014. Irons works with in-staff and Friends groups to develop programming and educates staff on appropriate marketing and licensing for film programs. She has presented on libraries and film programming at ALA in 2011 and at WLA conferences in 2011, 2012, and 2014.

© 2014 by the American Library Association

Printed in the United States of America
18 17 16 15 14   5 4 3 2 1

Extensive effort has gone into ensuring the reliability of the information in this book; however, the publisher makes no warranty, express or implied, with respect to the material contained herein.

ISBN: 978–0-8389–1197–6 (paper).

Library of Congress Cataloging-in-Publication Data

Irons, Kati.
Film programming for public libraries / Kati Irons.
     pages   cm
  Includes bibliographical references and index.
  ISBN 978-0-8389-1197-6 (alk. paper)
  1. Pierce County Library. 2. Motion picture film collections—Washington (State)—Pierce County. 3. Public libraries—Washington (State)—Pierce County. 4. Public libraries—Washington (State)—Pierce County—Special collections—Motion pictures. 5. Public libraries—Washington (State)—Pierce County.—Special collections—Video recordings. I. Title.
  Z692.M9I76 2014
  025.2'873—dc23

                    2014004172

Cover design by Casey Bayer. Image © javarman/Shutterstock, Inc.
Text design by Kirstin Krutsch in the Chaparral Pro, Dub Tone, and ITC Franklin Gothic Std typefaces.

♾ This paper meets the requirements of ANSI/NISO Z39.48–1992 (Permanence of Paper).

This book is dedicated to three amazing librarians without whom I would not be a librarian: Pam Darling, who showed me the path; Cindy Cunningham, who opened the door; and Sharon Ufer Lavell, who gave me the keys. Thank you!

CONTENTS

PREFACE

Film programming is a natural fit with libraries, another tool in our storehouse of storytimes, book groups, and lectures. They are an opportunity to create programs that are educational, emotional, and silly. They are an opportunity to reach out to every age group and interest group. Everyone loves movies, and as we sail into cinema's second century as an art form, it's safe to say there are plenty of movies for us to love.

That said, film programming can seem more complicated than other kinds of programming libraries offer. How do you choose films to show? What equipment should you use? Are you following the correct rules for publicly showing films? How do you market your programs? Where do you begin?

For fourteen years I have worked as the development librarian for the Film and Music Collection at the Pierce County Library System (PCLS) in Washington State. When I began, we had a small but well-loved collection of VHS tapes, and now PCLS has a collection of over two hundred thousand DVDs and growing. Although I would like to claim that this is entirely because I'm great at my job, the truth is that the world of movies has never been more available or more affordable. Our collection is that big because the world of films available for libraries to buy is that big—and growing.

In addition to building the PCLS film collection, I am also responsible for maintaining the film licenses for the system, keeping them current and keeping our staff educated on how to create programs that work within the bounds the licenses allow us. Because of this, I know all the questions staff often have and the places where librarians can get lost or discouraged when trying to organize film programs.

The goal of this book is to help shine some light on challenging film programming areas, such as licensing, marketing, and equipment. It's also to show you where to find inspiration for your own film programs, film advisory, and film displays. Ultimately, your imagination is the only limit on the kinds of film programs you can offer, and I hope this book can give you the tools to set your imagination free.

Throughout the book I will offer various suggestions of film titles relating to the topics at hand. These suggestions are not intended to be exhaustive or even "the best," but they are meant to be choices I think could make good film programs, or could inspire you to think of your own. When listing films, I include the year it was made, the production company, and the rating. I include films from multiple rating levels, including R.

I have done my best to ensure that the films I list in this book are, as of this writing, in print and available for purchase from traditional library vendors or from reliable online resources. When the source is an online vendor, I have determined that it is available new (not used) and reasonably priced. In other words, if it is only available used from Amazon for $112, I consider that "not available." As of this writing, the Disney films I mention in this book are not "in the vault," as Disney describes their out-of-print stock, but I make no promises to the whims of the Mouse House.

Much help in researching this book has been given by John Fossett, head of Collection Development for Kitsap Regional Library. John and I have created several film advisory programs for the Washington Library Association (WLA) and ALA, and he has been invaluable in providing me with and pointing me to good resources for this book. You will see his name pop up often throughout these pages!

ACKNOWLEDGMENTS

would like to acknowledge the help and support of the Pierce County Library and its staff, whose enthusiasm for film has made my career and by extension this book possible. This book would not have been possible without the help of John Fossett, my partner in cinematic crime and amazing programs, and John's wonderful system, the Kitsap Regional Library.

I also would like to acknowledge some special individuals who kept me going through the challenging task of writing a book, including Lisa Bitney, Elise DeGuiseppi, Holly Gorski, Matt Lemanski, Georgia Lomax, Judy Nelson, and Lisa Oldoski. I'd like to thank the Puget Sound Collection Development group for prompt and generous responses to spontaneous film questions, and the lovely ladies of the Friday Writers Group, who helped hold my feet to the fire.

My family also made this entirely possible, by answering the phone every time I called to say, "What have I agreed to?" and by replying, "Nothing you aren't capable of!" Mom, Dad, Bev, Sarah, David, and Szilvia, you're the bomb-diggety. I would also like to acknowledge my grandma, Betty Lou Irons, who loved movies, the *TV Guide* crossword, and Robert Redford above all things, and showed me that a polite obsession with movies is a perfectly respectable pastime.

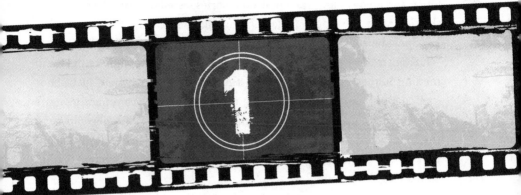

INTRODUCTION
Why Film Programming?

Visual-media programming has a long history in libraries. As a child I certainly remember filmstrips and 16 mm films being a regular part of my library experience. Media has long been a tool in the library programming toolbox, along with storytimes and book programming. Often libraries were able to offer movie experiences that customers were simply unable to get anywhere else.

Doug Roberts is a reference librarian who has worked for Spokane Public Library for forty years. In his role as the film and media specialist, he oversaw the 16 mm film collection for Spokane Public. Roberts says, "During the 1950s, '60s, '70s, and into the '80s, we had a large 16 mm film collection—over seven hundred titles. We also participated in the Washington Library Film Circuit (WLFC) and rotated packets of films monthly between libraries around the state. We loaned films to the public, teachers, senior centers, day cares, and elsewhere. In addition, we had regular weekly film showings at our downtown library auditorium."

In addition to weekly film showings, the Spokane Public Library hosted free noon-hour programs during the year that featured films or concerts. The audience included people who worked downtown, seniors, business-people, and other library regulars. People were encouraged to bring a brown-bag lunch and enjoy a film. The noon-hour series lasted for twenty years, until the closing of Spokane's old downtown branch in 1990.

Spokane didn't limit film showing to the library only. Roberts says, "Our Outreach Department would take films to retirement centers and nursing homes and show films to the residents somewhere just about every day on a monthly schedule. We also participated in community events and would set up library film showings for the public. These would be at the county fair, the Fourth of July parties or holiday parties at Riverfront Park, and especially, during the Expo '74 World's Fair, which was held in Spokane."

Spokane's collection was not limited to 16 mm film; 35 mm filmstrips with audio cassette soundtracks were available from the children's department for checkout, and helped serve local teachers and day-care centers. The library also had a few Dukane filmstrip viewers that staff could load for children to watch. "The tape would trigger the images to advance in the viewer on most," says Roberts, "although some were manual and needed to be advanced 'when you hear the beep'" (Doug Roberts, pers. comm.).

Through film, libraries had the opportunity to share content that was exclusive to library customers. Elise DeGuiseppi, who began her library career as a children's librarian in the late 1980s, says, "The short films we showed—[including] Weston Woods iconographic and animated adaptations of children's books [and] a bit of live action as well—were unique in that they weren't yet available on video (which was in its early days) and were not shown on TV. Libraries really were a market for these films." Of course, just as we have technical difficulties today, 16 mm film was not without its own quirks. "Children loved them," DeGuiseppi says, "but I lived in fear of threading and operating the projectors. One caught on fire once under my watch. While it was momentarily fascinating to see the film image being consumed by flames, I had to tear myself away from it for the sake of the children" (Elise DeGuiseppi, pers. comm.).

Many libraries had film and filmstrip collections, and some library systems created partnerships or consortia, such as the Washington Library Film Circuit (WLFC), to help make film—which could be quite expensive—more readily available. The WLFC was facilitated through the Washington State Library from the late 1950s through the 1970s. Member libraries received monthly packets of films, which helped expand their offerings to show and to circulate.

The advent of VHS changed the landscape of film for libraries. When VHS was first released, it was intended for the newly birthed rental market and came with a high price point. But consumers drove the market, demanding the ability to "own" their favorite movies and convincing the industry that there was a home-video market waiting to be tapped. Randy Pitman, publisher and editor of *Video Librarian*, was working for Kitsap (Wash.) Regional Library when the transition happened. "[When] home video hit in the mid-'80s," says Pitman, "acquisitions suddenly mushroomed from buying ten 16 mm films a year to eventually purchasing hundreds of VHS titles" (Randy Pitman, pers. comm.).

All libraries struggled with the question of whether or not to build VHS collections, and some decided no. Still more decided that if they did build a collection, it should be focused strictly on educational videos and perhaps classic films, but not a showcase for blockbusters or current popular films. Some believed that we must not allow this home-movie juggernaut to distract from the library's mission, which should be books.

On the one hand, never had libraries had greater access to almost any film they might want to show. On the other hand, our patrons were flush with the novelty of watching movies at home from their favorite chair and pausing when they wanted to run to the kitchen. The focus of libraries became helping patrons create individual viewing experiences, rather than create communal ones. "Ultimately, I think the wide availability of titles on video coupled with the arrival of big-screen TVs made [library] film programming a bit less special than in the days when you couldn't just immediately stream whatever title you felt like watching," says Pitman.

Libraries were stuck with how to show movies as well. VHS was designed to be watched on a TV screen. Expensive equipment might allow a system to show a movie on a bigger screen, but progress didn't bring to most libraries expensive screening equipment but instead the ubiquitous television sets with built-in VHS players. These might work adequately for a small group or a children's program, but showing a feature film to a crowded room on a 16-inch TV set simply did not work. And from our patrons' perspective, why should they come and sit in folding chairs in a crowded room to watch a movie they could watch at home? Libraries became movie suppliers, drifting out of the film programming business.

Other issues and questions arise each time we transition from one format to the next, such as the library community's role in preserving what the film industry itself is perhaps blithely discarding. Kate Mossman is the assistant library director for Everett (Wash.) Public Library and worked for the New York Public Library, where she offered many 16 mm film programs. Mossman says "There is so much from 16 mm that was never converted to VHS, and then so much of VHS never converted to DVD. It feels to me as if we are losing so much of film and TV history as people are now going to the Netflix/Hulu streaming model and [are] being satisfied with a few thousand titles" (Kate Mossman, pers. comm.).

It's true that nothing is ever static in libraries. Thanks to streaming video, libraries are facing another crossroads on the horizon when it comes to film. But also thanks to the high-quality picture of DVD and Blu-ray and readily available, inexpensive projection equipment, at this moment it has never been easier for a library to show films to groups large and small.

Our audience has evolved too. Watching movies at home is business as usual now. The idea of enjoying a film in community with others is a novelty. Economics is a very real issue for our customers. In 1980—the year VHS trumped Beta to become the winner of the home-video market—the average cost of a movie ticket was $2.89. In 2012 the national average cost of a ticket was $8.12 (although it's $10.50 at the movie theater down the street from me!).

Even taking inflation into account, there's a huge difference in taking a family of four out to the movies for $40 instead of $12. Going out to the movies is something many families can manage rarely, if at all, but they still want to find inexpensive, entertaining activities to do as a family. Single adults and couples want to find social activities that don't involve spending money at bars or restaurants. Senior citizens need activities that aren't hard on their wallets.

The idea of the "third place" has taken hold of the library imagination in recent years. Communities need a place—a not-work, not-home place—where they can gather, socialize, relax, retreat, and recharge. In recent decades that third-place location has become dominated by commercial enterprises such as coffeehouses and Internet cafes. But libraries are natural places for the community to gather, and unlike commercial enterprises, they are supported by the public good, and free to the individual. "Libraries have become one of the last bastions of community gathering," says Randy Pitman, "so in that respect, film programming does remain somewhat special."

CREATING YOUR FILM PROGRAM

Putting together a film program can be as easy as putting out some chairs, popping a movie in, and hoping that your audience has a good time. It can also be something more than that. I believe you'll find that the more thoughtful planning you put into your film programs, the more your patrons will enjoy them, and you will enjoy the benefits of a popular program. The first step in this process is to identify your audience.

The more you know about the audience you hope to attract to your film program, the better that program is going to go. Age is usually one of the first determiners of the kind of film you want to show, when you're going to show it and how to promote it.

For the purposes of this book I have focused on the following age groups:

- young children (2 to 5 years)
- children (5–10), tweens (11–13), and families*
- teens (14–17) and young adults
- adults (18+)
- seniors (65+)

*I've included "families" in the list above to acknowledge the fact that many of our patrons are in need of family programming—programs that will appeal to everyone from a 5-year-old to Grandma.

Film Programs for Young Children

Anyone who does storytimes already knows there's a world of difference between programs for 2-year-olds and for 6-year-olds. Organizing a children's movie time with a family film may bring all these groups together, and general enjoyment will likely be had by all.

If, on the other hand, you want to focus a film program specifically for younger children, you're probably going to want to think "short," for short attention spans and wiggly bodies. Live Oak, Westin Woods, and Spoken Arts are all companies that produce storybooks on DVD, which can be a fun way to spice up storytimes or to provide a storytime when you are short of staff.

Animals are always a winner with kids of all ages, but there are some animal series made just for kids, such as *The World of Baby Animals*, *Animal Atlas*, *Puppy Party*, and, of course, its sister production, *Kitten Party*. National Geographic has a wide assortment of animal-related DVDs for kids, including the Really Wild Animals series.

Nick Jr. produces a wide array of DVD programming that is fun for young kids, such as *Bubble Guppies Dora the Explorer*, *Go, Diego, Go!*, *Pocoyo*, and *Yo Gabba Gabba!* PBS Kids has *Arthur*, *Caillou*, *Dinosaur Train*, and *Sid the Science Kid*. NCircle Entertainment is a children's programming producer that creates shows that are shown on several different networks including PBS, Nick Jr., and NBC Kids. Some NCircle shows are *The Cat in the Hat Knows a Lot about That!*, *Dino Dan*, *Jim Henson's Pajanimals*, *Octonauts*, *Sid the Science Kid*, and *The Wiggles*.

Kids enjoy music, dancing, and running around. Many kids shows have a strong musical component. *Sesame Street* has a *Kids' Favorite Songs* DVD series, and *Angelina Ballerina Dance around the World* (2013; Hit Entertainment, NR) features dances from Ireland to China. Other music and movement-heavy DVD series include *Bear in the Big Blue House*, *Classical Baby*, *The Monkey Doos*, and *Wee Sing*.

Of course, kids today are pretty saturated with TV at home, so it might be fun to show them some "classic" stuff they have yet to be introduced to, such as *The Animated Tales of the World*; *Fractured Fairy Tales*; *Fraggle Rock*;

and Looney Tunes, Hanna-Barbera, Pink Panther, and Rocky & Bullwinkle cartoons.

Certainly, if you're showing a song-and-dance DVD to your group, all the kids will be up and moving; however, the attention span for watching videos varies from child to child. One thing to consider is whether, in addition to showing a video, you also want to make available quiet toys—such as building blocks, Legos, or coloring—for kids whose attention spans wander when videos are on, or who are kinesthetic and need to keep moving even if they're interested in the video. It all depends on how much controlled chaos you're comfortable with!

PROGRAMMING TIP
What to Do with Those under 2?

You'll notice that in the age groups under "children," I started with the age of 2, although most libraries have programs for younger children. I left out children under the age of 2 on purpose in discussing film programming.

The American Association of Pediatrics has recommended that children under the age of 2 should not be exposed to television or video viewing.[1] At this young age, children benefit best from direct interaction with parents or caregivers for healthy brain development. There have been studies that suggest exposure to television or video for the very young may interfere with language development or even contribute to the development of ADHD, although these studies have not been conclusive. Regardless, children younger than 2 learn best with one-on-one human interaction.

Some insist that children should not be exposed to television or video at all but most experts agree that after the age of 2, limited television or video time (no more than one to two hours a day) which is supervised by an adult (as opposed to "parking" in front of the screen) is OK.[2] The most important aspect of how much children will benefit or not from video viewing is how much human interaction goes along with it. Ultimately children learn much more from people than from screens.

Film Programs for Children, Tweens, and Families

Film programming for older children opens the door to the world of family films, cartoons, television shows and even family friendly documentaries. The problem really isn't finding something to show as much as it is narrowing the field! The more you know about your audience, the more successful your programs will be. This can mean trying a few different programs and finding out what works.

Tami Masenhimer is a supervisor for a library branch in Fife, Washington. She includes films in the rotation of events for Fife's "First Tuesday" program: "The First Tuesday of every month we have some kind of program. It may be a puppet show or storyteller or a movie. We always pick a 'new release' DVD, something that has just come out. It's how we promote the film program." The audience for the films is mixed, with some younger kids, but also "we always have a small group of teen boys who spend a lot of time at the library."

One thing Masenhimer learned quickly is while all the kids, including the teens, enjoyed the G-rated family movies she was showing, for whatever reason, cartoons or animated films didn't hold their interest. For this reason, when selecting DVDs to show, she leans toward live-action family films rather than animated ones. This is a trial-and-error process. I'm not suggesting that kids don't like cartoons—of course they do. But Masenhimer learned that in her community kids were more interested in live action.

As the person who needs to wade through the vast sea of films and choose the ones that will be successful for a kids' movie program, where do you start? You can use the usual film resources, such as IMDB or Amazon, to identify what's coming out and what's popular. But how do you evaluate it before you show it to your community? There are a number of online resources available that offer family-friendly reviews that can be excellent tools to help you decide how a particular film may fly in your community.

Kids-In-Mind (www.kids-in-mind.com) is an interesting tool in that it does not review films in the sense of "good" or "bad," or make any kind of critical assessment of the films featured on the site. What it does do for each reviewed film is grade it in three categories: Violence, Sex & Nudity, and Profanity. Further, it actually details the actions or scenes which trigger grades in the various categories.

So, for example, the film *The Dark Knight Rises* is given a rank of 2 for Sex & Nudity, 7 for Violence, and 3 for Profanity. We can also learn that the 2 for Sex & Nudity was earned in part for "a scene of prolonged kissing" and "a woman wearing a tight leather jumpsuit through the film."

The purpose of Kids-In-Mind, as explained by the creators, is to help parents navigate the sometimes vague rating system. A film may be PG, but what does that PG *mean*? As a librarian, I am, on the one side, always wary of suggesting ways to parse or label films; but on the other, when you are showing films, it's nice to have a tool that helps you know what you're in for.

"They tend to rate things much more strictly than I would," says one librarian with whom I spoke who regularly uses Kids-In-Mind, "so it's like peeking into the mind of the 'worst case scenario' unhappy parent. If Kids-In-Mind rates a film as 3 or less in the three categories, I feel pretty confident that no one is going to be unhappy."

Commonsense Media (www.commonsensemedia.org) is a national nonpartisan advocacy organization that studies the effects of media on children and families. They review all kinds of media, not just films, including television, video games, websites, books, and music.

Unlike Kids-In-Mind, Commonsense Media does review films in the classic sense of whether the reviewer thinks the film is good or bad or boring or piffle or gross or pointless or awesome. It also provides a few different methods of ranking films, which can be useful in designing film programs. The first is an age ranking. Commonsense Media gives each film an age number indicating the appropriate age for the film. So, for example, Commonsense Media gave the 2012 film *The Three Stooges*, which has an MPAA rating of PG, an age-appropriateness score of 9. The age score also indicates that it may be appropriate for kids as young as 8 "with caution," and that Commonsense Media does not recommend the film at all for children 7 or younger.

Commonsense Media also provides breakdown scores in detailed categories: Positive Messages, Positive Role Models, Violence, Sex, Language, Consumerism, and Drinking, Drugs, & Smoking.

Finally, Commonsense Media provides links to "viewalikes" picked by their editors. In the case of the aforementioned *Three Stooges*, they recommend *The Nutty Professor* from 1963 and Buster Keaton's classic *Steamboat Bill Jr.* They also link to film lists, which in the case of *The Three Stooges* include "Guy Movies: Our Favorite Goofballs" and "Best Comedy Classic Films."

For helping you design programs, Commonsense Media gives you tools to decide if you're targeting the right movie to the program's age group. The "viewalike" lists can also be extremely helpful in inspiring ideas for new programs.

Parent Previews (www.parentpreviews.com) is a website as well as a national syndicated newspaper column and radio show, all of which focus on providing parents more information on family films. Unlike most of the other resources on this list, Parent Previews does not review R-rated films, focusing only on G, PG, and PG-13 films.

Parent Previews uses an A through D grading system, with *A* reflecting a title they feel is both entertaining and enriching and *D* indicating a film they do not believe is appropriate for family viewing. Every film is given an overall grade, and then additional grades in Violence, Sexual Content, Language, and Drugs & Alcohol. The overall grade is an average of the category grades.

PluggedIn (www.pluggedin.com) is a film-review site for parents created by Focus on the Family, a conservative evangelical nonprofit organization. It offers detailed reviews of titles, which offer analysis based on categories such as Positive Elements, Spiritual Content, Sexual Content, Violent Content, Crude or Profane Language, Drug and Alcohol Content, and Other Negative Elements.

The reviews are very detailed and reflect a conservative Christian perspective. Depending on the community that you serve, reviews from PluggedIn could be very helpful in identifying good film choices for your programs.

Other issues come up with family and children's programs beyond choosing a film, all of which are things you should think through beforehand to minimize surprises.

Is there an age limit, either high or low? Do you want kids to be at least 5 or not older than 10? Make sure you say so in the publicity.

Is it OK for parents to drop their kids off and come back to pick them up? Do you want all children to be accompanied by a parent or caregiver, or perhaps children under a certain age?

"Family films" tend to be open to anyone, but children's film times are generally like a children's storytime: you assume the audience is going to be children and their caregivers. Is any adult in attendance required to have a child with them?

These are the sorts of questions that often don't matter at all, until suddenly they do matter.

When I started this book, I asked some of my colleagues to send me feedback on any interesting experiences of lessons they had learned while doing film programming. Patty Amador, who works at the University Place Branch of the Pierce County Library, had this experience about running a family film program to share:

> I offered popcorn to attract people to my first movie. I had an entire Costco-size box of popcorn. I popped enough for everyone to have a coffee filter of popcorn (used what I had at the

time!) and then left the room. When I returned about ten minutes before the movie was out, all the popcorn was popped by two moms. There was a line of ten people waiting for their own bag. So it went from everyone getting a coffee filter to everyone getting a bag. Now I just tell them that they can bring their own snacks.

Which brings me to the lesson learned: Always have someone in charge of the room! This could be a volunteer or staff person or yourself. People can't be left alone in a room for two hours without some kind of problem. And never leave anything unattended in the room.

Movie Ideas for Children, Tween, and Family Film Programs

Amazing Animals

Born Free (1966; Columbia TriStar, PG)
Winged Migration (2003; Columbia TriStar, G)
March of the Penguins (2005; Warner Home Video, G)
African Cats (2011; Disneynature, G)

Classic Disney Live Action

The Parent Trap (1961)
Mary Poppins (1964)
Bedknobs and Broomsticks (1971)
Pete's Dragon (1977)

Fantasy Adventure Films for Kids

Time Bandits (1981; Image Entertainment, PG)
Dark Crystal (1982; Columbia TriStar, PG)
Labyrinth (1986; Columbia TriStar, PG)
Indian in the Cupboard (1995; Columbia TriStar, PG)

Princess Movies That Don't Suck

The Princess Bride (1987; MGM, PG)
Anastasia (1997; 20th Century Fox, G)
Ella Enchanted (2004; Miramax, PG)
Frozen (2014; Disney, PG)

Sports

The Mighty Ducks (1992; Disney, PG)
Rudy (1993; Columbia TriStar, PG)
Sandlot (1993; 20th Century Fox, PG)
She's the Man (2006; DreamWorks Pictures, PG-13)

Summertime Movies

The Bad News Bears (1976; Paramount, PG)
Goonies (1985; Warner Home Video, PG)
Heavyweights (1995; Disney, PG)
Diary of a Wimpy Kid: Dog Days (2012; 20th Century Fox, PG)

Superhero Movies for Kids

Spy Kids (2001; Dimension Home Video, PG)
The Incredibles (2004; Disney, PG)
Sky High (2005; Disney, PG)
Zoom: Academy for Superheroes (2006; Sony, PG)

In addition to these suggestions, appendix A has a list of family films based on children's literature.

PROGRAMMING TIP
Make It a Bedtime Movie!

Plan a family film time in the early evening and encourage attendees to bring blankets and pillows and to wear their pj's! Consider showing films related to bedtime stories.

Film Programs for Teens and Young Adults

Teen programming is perhaps one of the more challenging areas for deciding what to show. On the one hand, teens really like movies, so picking films should be like choosing raw meat for hungry tigers. Throw anything in the pen and they ought to enjoy it.

But teens are teens. They like everything. They like only what they like. They like what all their friends like, but they only like unique stuff that

PROGRAMMING TIP
Coordinate a System-Wide Film Program around a Theme

In fall 2011, the new feature film *The Muppets* was released to theaters. In anticipation of this sure-to-be-popular release, the Youth Services Department of the Pierce County Library decided to organize a system-wide film program promoted under the title "It's the Muppets." New copies of all the previous Muppet films were purchased on DVD, and branches reserved the title or titles they wished to show during the month of November.

The branches benefited from system-wide coordinated publicity but also were able to put their own unique touches on their Muppet programs. In addition to showing a Muppet film, several branches also offered a Muppet-themed craft. For those branches showing *Muppet Treasure Island*, attendees were encouraged to dress like pirates.

The Muppet films provided an excellent inspiration for this program, as unlike many other popular family film characters, their films are not a "series" per se (it's not *Muppets I, Muppets II: The Revenge of Kermit, Muppets III,* etc.), but instead related by the same characters.

everyone else hates. Researching films for teens is a singularly frustrating experience. There are dozens, if not hundreds of films about teens and starring teens, and certainly "teen films for teens" is a ripe place to come up with ideas for films teens will enjoy.

The mistake comes though when we stop there. Teens are almost adults. In cultures other than ours, they *are* adults. They care about what adults care about. They care about love and money and death and war and sex. They're interested in the world around them. They don't like to feel patronized.

This is a dilemma that librarians serving teens experience with all materials, but particularly with movies where society's official designation of "age appropriateness" is stamped so clearly on the box. The best teen film festival in the world, according to most teens, would feature a lot of R-rated films. Not because teens are obsessed only with the prurient, but because a lot of R-rated films are really interesting. They're about the aforementioned love and money and death and war and sex.

As I cover in chapter 6, "Legalities and Related Issues," ratings are informational. They're not "law," but for teen programs, I'd be doing a lousy job if I told you that you shouldn't pay attention to ratings when choosing such films. This book, I hope, is a guide to helping you establish successful lasting film programs, not notorious film programs that lead to community uproar.

Ultimately the most successful teen programs are those that take into account the wants and needs of the teens at your particular library. I will say that I believe you can show almost anything and everything to teens, including classics, rom-coms, action, drama or foreign, and have a successful program. However, your teens—the teens you are programming for—may snooze at the sight of a black-and-white film, may flee from musicals, or scoff at "teen" movies. They may enthusiastically demand a Kurosawa film festival and then forget to show up.

Or, like hungry tigers, they may enthusiastically devour everything you throw at them!

Resources are available to help get ideas for teen programs. Commonsense Media, which I discussed in the children's section, has solid tools to help evaluate and find films for teens. In fact, you can even click on the age of your audience—say, 15, for example—and be delivered an extensive list of films Commonsense Media has evaluated as appropriate for that age.

In 2005, the British Film Institute, which regularly publishes lists such as "The Greatest Films of All Time" and "The Greatest Directors of All Time," published a list of "The 50 Films You Should See by the Age of 14."[3] The list is an interesting mix of older and more modern films, and includes titles from around the world. It's actually quite a fascinating list, although I doubt most children would be able to get to all of these by the age of 14.

The list itself generated some controversy when it was published.[4] Some accused it of being dreary and failing to offer uplift. Some accused the BFI of confusing films *about* children and teens (sometimes in terrible situations) with films *for* teens. Some felt there were strange omissions—a complete lack of war films, for example, even though war, both historical and present day, is a topic of interest to teens.

Although the purpose of the list is identifying films children should see before the age of 14, I think the mix of titles on the list could provide very interesting fodder for a teen program. It's probably the only film list you're ever going to find that includes *Back to the Future*, *Au Revoir Les Enfants*, *Edward Scissorhands*, and *Night of the Hunter*.

ALA teen organization YALSA is also a very good source for ideas of movies for teens. Every year YALSA produces a list of films based around a single theme. Recent themes have included Survival, Song & Dance, Rebellion & Conformity, Coming of Age around the World, and Other Times/ Other Places. Current and past lists are available on the YALSA website.[5]

Anime!

One cannot talk about film programs for teens without discussing anime. Anime has gone from a rare and mysterious import to a vital part of the popular culture mainstream. It's also something your teens may know more about than you do, which can make choosing what to show nerve-racking.

My first advice for organizing an anime program for teens is asking your teens what they like. This will help you learn what's out there and what the interest level is in your community. Once you've gotten the nitty-gritty from your teens, there are other resources at your disposal that can help you identify good anime films and series for programs.

I feel like I keep visiting the same well, but once again **Commonsense Media** is a great resource. They have lists of anime series and films that evaluate based on age and give you a sense of content you may need to consider.

To help you keep up with what's happening in the world of anime, I recommend **Anime News Network** (www.animenewsnetwork.com). You'll find news, new releases, and articles about the worlds of anime and manga.

Anime Planet (www.animeplanet.com) is another resource for reviews and articles about anime and manga. Understand that in the case of both Anime News Network and Anime Planet, when I say "reviews," I mean impassioned and lengthy essays about every single minute detail of the anime in question. This is not to suggest the reviews are fawning. On the contrary, some of them are quite harsh for reasons sometimes not immediately clear. However, like learning a foreign language, sometimes immersion is the best place to start.

One question that often arises when dealing with anime programs is, of course, whether the anime you wish to show is covered under your licenses. Movie Licensing USA offers a special "Anime License" that covers products from FUNimation Entertainment, which includes series such as *Ah! My Goddess*, *Dragon Ball Z*, *Fullmetal Alchemist*, and hundreds more. Another option—which I wouldn't recommend for most movies, but enthusiastically recommend for anime—is to contact the producer of the anime series directly. Many anime producers will give you permission to show their programs at no charge and are often happy to hear from libraries.

It can take time, patience, good marketing, and good word of mouth to get a teen anime group going. Alexander Byrne, a youth services librarian for Pierce County Library, shared the following experience working on a teen anime program:

> I inherited an anime club from a coworker upon coming into my position. I was a pretty knowledgeable anime guy, so I thought I would have no problem at all attracting hordes upon hordes of teens to talk anime.
>
> After a few months, I discontinued the anime club for lack of attendance. Not that we weren't having a blast when we had people there. But an anime club meeting only once a month, on a Friday afternoon, didn't spark a lot of retention in the ranks. It also took a very long time to get through any twenty-six-episode series.
>
> The other thing I didn't really do that much was advertise, and yes, I can hear the facepalms that are happening right now. I tried to get the people who were coming to spread the word by word of mouth, but they didn't do a whole lot when they remembered, and I never did get any flyers in the school. Considering the fact that the library is one of plenty of other afterschool things to be doing, after a while, everybody sort of moved on.
>
> Sometimes, I guess, you just have to know your community. And advertise.

Movie Ideas for Teens and Young Adult Film Programs

Anime Movies

Porco Rosso (1992; Touchstone, PG)
Gintama: The Movie (2010; Sentai, 13Up)
Children Who Chase Lost Voices (2011; Sentai, 13Up)
Summer Wars (2011; NTV, 13Up)

Horror Movies

Jaws (1975; Universal, PG)
Poltergeist (1982; Warner Home Video, PG)
Gremlins (1984; Warner Home Video, PG)
Tremors (1989; Universal, PG-13)

PROGRAMMING TIP
Let Tour Teens Submit or Vote on Film Ideas

A great way to get your teens involved in film programs is to give them the option of submitting and/or voting on films to see. I heard an anecdote from one librarian about her experience with this which offers food for thought. She offered her teens the chance to "Vote on Your Favorite '80s Teen Movie," which seemed like a winner. The '80s were certainly a golden age of teen films! But she was confronted with a lot of blank stares, and the sinking realization that none of her teens had actually been alive in the '80s, obviously. Asking them to identify an '80s teen movie was like (admitting my age here) asking my generation to identify our favorite '60s teen movie. (Um, *West Side Story*?)

When the poll was made more specific—asking them to choose their favorite John Hughes movie—the teens were thrilled and voted away. John Hughes they knew all about. But putting them on the spot to pick what was, from their perspective, a "classic movie" (ouch!) did not go so well.

The advent of home video has actually given kids today the opportunity to be fairly savvy about movies from all ages, but sometimes we may need to work with them a little to learn what their access points are.

I'm With the Band

Eddie and the Cruisers (1983; MGM, PG-13)
La Bamba (1986; Columbia TriStar, PG)
Across the Universe (2007; Columbia, PG-13)
Rock of Ages (2012; Warner Bros., PG-13)

It Came From the Video Game Console

Mortal Kombat (1995; New Line Cinema, PG-13)
Final Fantasy (2001; Columbia TriStar, PG-13)
Lara Croft: Tomb Raider (2001; Paramount, PG-13)
Prince of Persia: The Sands of Time (2010; Disney, PG-13)

Need for Speed

Bullitt (1968; Warner Home Video, PG)
Days of Thunder (1990; Paramount, PG-13)
Talladega Nights (2006; Sony, PG-13)
Fast & Furious (2009; Universal, PG-13)

Originals and Remakes

The Mummy (1932; Universal, NR; and 1999; Universal, PG-13)

Invasion of the Body Snatchers (1956; Olive Films, NR; and 1978; MGM, PG)

The Italian Job (1969; Paramount, G; and 2003; Paramount, PG-13)

Rear Window (1954; Universal, PG) and *Disturbia* (2007; Paramount, PG-13)

Rockumentaries

The Beatles' *Help!* (1965; Capitol, NR) and *Yellow Submarine* (1968; Apple Films, NR)

Gimme Shelter (1970; Criterion, NR)

Stop Making Sense (1984; Palm, NR)

I Am Trying to Break Your Heart (2002; Plexifilm, NR)

Saving the World through the Power of Dance

West Side Story (1961; 20th Century Fox, NR)

Footloose (1984; Paramount, PG; and 2011; Paramount, PG-13)

Dirty Dancing (1987; Lions Gate, PG-13)

Stomp the Yard (2007; Columbia TriStar, PG-13)

Teens of Yore

Rebel without a Cause (1955; Warner Home Video, NR)

Bye Bye Birdie (1963; Columbia TriStar, G)

The Outsiders (1983; Warner Home Video, PG)

Sixteen Candles (1984; Universal, PG)

Film Programs for Adults

For the sake of clarity in our discussions, let's agree that "adult film" does not mean porn but rather a film that will be of interest to an adult audience. "Adult film programs" means programs for adults from 18 to 180. I will also discuss film programming for seniors in more detail later in the chapter.

For adult film programs, the world is your oyster. But it's daunting, narrowing down the world of film to find good choices. There are plenty of film review resources—both online and in good old-fashioned book form—that are great to learn more about films once you have some in mind. But where do you start when you don't know where to start?

Film Organizations

The American Film Institute (www.afi.com) is a nonprofit organization dedicated to preserving the history of film and educating future filmmakers and filmgoers. They also produce and promote lists of films that slice and dice films in an amazing array of access points. "100 Years . . . 100 Movies" is a juried list of the "top 100" films of all time, which AFI updates approximately every ten years. AFI also has lists featuring comedy ("100 Laughs"), thrillers ("100 Thrills"), romances ("100 Passions"), and inspirational ("100 Cheers"). They have lists of great musicals, of movies with great songs, of "heroes and villains," and of great movie quotes.

That each list features one hundred titles is both a strength and a weakness, depending on what you want to use the lists for. For the purposes of looking for film programming inspiration it's fantastic, because you're going to see a lot of titles. For the purposes of identifying truly great films, well, in a list of one hundred great titles, there are a few that aren't really *that* great. In addition, AFI's focus is American cinema, so you're not going to see too many non-American films on these lists, no matter how classic they may be.

Perhaps in response to the criticism that "100 Top Films" in any genre begins to seem meaningless once you get toward the bottom, AFI has also created the "10 Top 10" lists. These are the top ten films in ten genres,

PROGRAMMING TIP
Use Your Calendar!

It's easy to forget that the entire calendar can provide enough inspiration to take care of all your film programming. Sure, it's easy to remember to pull out holiday films in December, Black History Month films in February, and even patriotic films in July, but did you know that April 25 is National Penguin Awareness Day? Can you think of a better reason to show *March of the Penguins*? May is National Guide Dog Appreciation Month! Lassie wasn't exactly a guide dog, but she sure rescued lots of people from wells. Granted, you might struggle with finding an appropriate film for National Pickle Day (November 14), but November is also National Novel Writing Month—a great time to pull out *Capote* or *The Hours* or *Adaptation* or any of the other many great films about writers struggling to write. Appendix B provides a yearlong list of film ideas inspired by the calendar to use as a starting point in developing your own.

including animation, romantic comedy, western, sports, gangster, and even courtroom drama.

It can be easy to slip into arguing mode with these lists. *Kramer vs. Kramer* is a better courtroom drama than *A Few Good Men?* Really? I mean, *really*?! But remember what we're after. We're busy librarians looking for good film program ideas. Take AFI's "Top 10 Courtroom Dramas" list and viola, you have a Courtroom Drama Film Series, and your *patrons* can argue over whether *Kramer vs. Kramer* is better than *A Few Good Men.*

The British Film Institute, which I mentioned earlier in the teen discussion, also has similar lists with broader content. The BFI lists include many more international films than the AFI lists and— not to be too judgmental toward the AFI—there's a certain gravitas to the BFI lists that the AFI lists lack, for better or worse.

The American Library Association Video Round Table

The American Library Association Video Round Table (VRT) is a group dedicated to the advocacy of video within libraries. Every year since 1998, the VRT has produced a "Notable Videos for Adults" list that identifies the best educational, performance, and how-to videos from the previous year, as selected by a VRT committee.

The lists are a great resource for information, particularly for great documentaries. The lists are available on the ALA website on the "Video Round Table (VRT)" page (www.ala.org/vrt/front).

Film Festivals

The Sundance Film Festival is now famous for reintroducing the American public to independent cinema. The Sundance Film Festival website (www .sundance.org/festival), in addition to having news about the latest independent films coming soon to a festival or theater near you, has a searchable and browsable archive of each festival back to 1984. If you're searching for a good independent film or documentary, this is a good resource. It's also, back to my earlier statement about the AFI lists, a quick-and-dirty film program idea. Have a mini Sundance Film Festival with films featured at Sundance through the years.

Film festival websites are a great place to get ideas for films and film programs. Many sites have a history section that shows winners of previous years. Many festivals have year-round programming that features classic, independent, and foreign films that are in wide release. Unless you are in the position to be directly competing with the festival (which would be tacky), I think borrowing their ideas is a fantastic one. Festivals are run by people who know film and are incredibly passionate about it. Many film festival sites include archives of past-year programs that are a treasure trove of film ideas.

A few of the many film festivals that have good resources for great program ideas are:

American Black Film Festival: http://abff.com/festival
AFI (American Film Institute) Fest: www.afi.com/afifest
Aspen FilmFest: www.aspenfilm.org
BFI (British Film Institute) Film Festival: www.bfi.org.uk/lff
Ebertfest (formerly known as "Roger Ebert's Overlooked Film Festival"): www.ebertfest.com
Edinburgh International Film Festival: www.edfilmfest.org.uk
Full Frame Documentary Film Festival: www.fullframefest.org
Los Angeles Film Festival: www.lafilmfest.com
New York Asian Film Festival: www.subwaycinema.com
San Diego Latino Film Festival: www.sdlatinofilm.com
Seattle International Film Festival: www.siff.net/index.aspx
Telluride: www.telluridefilmfestival.org and its sister organization Telluride Year Round: http://tffyearround.wordpress.com
Toronto International Film Festival: http://tiff.net
Tribeca: www.tribecafilm.com
Vancouver International Film Festival: www.viff.org/festival

The Critics

Film critics are thick on the ground and on the Internet these days. However there was a time, back in the time of dinosaurs, when there weren't quite so many, and there were a few who actually became famous. These were critics who made or broke films, who dined with directors, and haunted movie screenings like the Angels of Death and Mercy.

Some of these critics are still with us, and some have passed on, but what's true about this select few is that they know a lot about film. Some of them have web presences today, and several of them have published books. If you're looking for ideas for programs or even just an easy, manageable film education, brush up on the works of these critics.

Roger Ebert—One of the first things I learned as a fresh-faced young librarian is that Roger Ebert is controversial in certain circles, due in part to his youthful foray into screenwriting on the 1970 Russ Meyer film *Beyond the Valley of the Dolls*. I offer this not to discourage you from studying his film criticism, but as context so that you are not caught off-guard (as I was when I offered a patron a Roger Ebert book and was accused of peddling porn).

This caution aside, Ebert was one of the more prolific film critics of the last forty years. He published dozens of books, including his annual series *Roger Ebert's Movie Yearbook* and his Great Movies series. Ebert's *The Great Movies* is intended to be, as Ebert says in the introduction to volume I, "not the greatest movies of all time, because all lists of great movies are a foolish attempt to codify works which must stand alone, but it's fair to say if you want a tour of the landmarks of cinema, start here."[6]

Perversely, my personal favorite of Roger Ebert's series is his collections of reviews for his least favorite films of all time. The first in this series is *I Hated, Hated, Hated This Movie*, and the most recent edition is *A Horrible Experience of Unbearable Length*. I'm not sure what audience would be up for it, but personally I would love to do a film program of films that Roger Ebert hates, complete with popcorn to throw at the screen. If you're brave enough to try it, please let me know how it goes!

Although Ebert is no longer with us, his website www.rogerebert.com continues to provide a wealth of information on classic and current movies. The site contains an extensive collection of Ebert's film reviews, essays, and analysis. It is also regularly updated by a group of film experts chosen by Ebert and his wife who provide current film reviews, analysis and commentary.

David Denby—David Denby is a film critic for the *New Yorker* magazine, a position he shares with the critic Anthony Lane. Before coming to work at the *New Yorker*, he was the film critic for *New York Magazine*. Denby's 2012 book *Do The Movies Have a Future?* is a collection of his reviews, essays, and ponderings about the history and future of cinema.

Denby's reviews are also archived on the *New Yorker* website, although one must be a subscriber to access complete versions of more than his most recent essays. His older reviews, which he wrote for *New York Magazine*, are available in their entirety on the *New York Magazine* website (http://nymag.com/nymag/author_390).

David Edelstein—David Edelstein is the chief film critic for *New York Magazine* and film critic for the NPR program *Fresh Air* as well as *CBS Sun-*

day Morning. As a reviewer he has also worked for *Slate, Esquire, Rolling Stone,* and a long list of newspaper and magazine publications.

Many of Edelstein's reviews and essays are available on the Internet. *New York Magazine* has archived his reviews back to 2006 as well as his blog *The Projectionist* (http://nymag.com/daily/movies). His annual "Top 10 Films of the Year" lists are available on the *Slate* and NPR websites.

Edelstein is a plain, no-nonsense reviewer, rarely given to philosophical rumination. He's happy to give blockbuster films good reviews if he enjoyed them, and he's not afraid to voice his displeasure at films that have become critical darlings. His "Ten Best of the Year" lists are always a good mix of known and not-so-well-known films and documentaries of the year, and often brazenly missing the big films that are always on "everyone's" lists.

Anthony Lane—Anthony Lane has been the film critic for the *New Yorker* magazine since 1993. In addition to his reviews, which tend to be some of the more pithy and oft-quoted reviews out there, Lane also writes essays for the *New Yorker* on film and literature, including analyses of important films and film people, such as Alfred Hitchcock and Buster Keaton.

Nobody's Perfect, a collection of Lane's most memorable reviews to date, was published in 2002 and fans of his work certainly hope another one will be soon. The *New Yorker* website provides an archive of his work, though again, one must subscribe to access more than the most recent reviews.

Pauline Kael—When film reviewers discuss the film reviewer who inspired them the most, they are usually talking about Pauline Kael. Kael was the film reviewer for the *New Yorker* from 1968 to 1991 and in many respects invented the informal, conversational essay form of review that is commonplace today.

Kael was opinionated and brash, with no concern about eviscerating films other reviewers found great. In her review for *The Sound of Music* she referred to it as "The Sound of Money" and accused it of being "a sugar coated lie that people seem to want to eat."[7] Kael was a champion of many of the young directors of 1970s cinema, waxing ecstatic about films like *M*A*S*H* and *Bonnie and Clyde*—which, though undoubtedly classics today, were frankly befuddling to many of the old guard of reviewers at the time.

Kael's reviews and interviews are collected in many books, including *The Age of Movies: Selected Writings of Pauline Kael, For Keeps: 30 Years at the Movies,* and *I Lost It at the Movies,* to name but a small few.

Leonard Maltin—Leonard Maltin is most well-known for his annual *Leonard Maltin's Movie Guide,* phone book–thick guides of capsule reviews of thousands of films, which have been published annually since 1978. Maltin also has a website, http://blogs.indiewire.com/leonardmaltin, which includes reviews of current and classic films as well as film-related articles and interviews.

Maltin has written several books about specific film eras and genres, including *Of Mice and Magic: A History of American Animated Cartoons*, *The Little Rascals: The Life and Times of Our Gang* and *Leonard Maltin's Classic Movie Guide*. He also wrote *Leonard Maltin's 151 Best Movies You've Never Seen*, a compilation of reviews of some of Maltin's favorite films that came and went without a trace.

Steven Jay Schneider—Schneider is admittedly not a film critic like the others on this list. He is instead a film scholar who has written several books on film that provide a thorough look a mainstream, cult, and underground cinema. He is most well-known for editing *1001 Films You Must See Before You Die*, but has also edited books on horror, science fiction, and world cinema, as well as *501 Movie Directors: A Comprehensive Guide to the Greatest Film Directors*.

John Simon—John Simon is a quadruple threat in the reviewing industry, known for his theater, film, book, and music reviews. He became known for his savage theater reviews, which spare no one's feelings and make him something of a pariah in certain circles, which is not necessarily a bad thing for a critic. In reviewing film, he carries the same challenging tone as in his theater reviews, with much name checking of Shakespeare and exasperated longing for the "golden era" of cinema.

He is, in a rather amusing way, the stereotypical crotchety critic. In his review for the film *Terms of Endearment*, Simon says: "Television, like a reverse Falstaff, is not only witless in itself, but also the cause of witlessness in other fields it has contaminated,"[8] which is as succinct a summation of the kind of reviewer Simon is as any.

Simon has worked as a critic since the early 1960s and continues writing to this day on his website John Simon Uncensored (http://uncensoredsimon .blogspot.com), the name of which is a deliberate jab at *New York Magazine*, where he worked for almost forty years, and Bloomberg Media, with whom he parted ways in 2005.

Simon has a number of books, including *John Simon on Film: Criticism 1982–2001*. His articles and reviews are also archived on the *New York Magazine* website (http://nymag.com/nymag/author_379).

In recommending a look at the work—including older work—of reviewers, I'm not suggesting that you should read, like, and agree with everything they say. Some of the enjoyment in reading reviews, to my mind, is violently disagreeing with them. But I do find that reading the works of reviewers is a cheap and easy way to get a film education. Critics invariably mention other films, directors, and actors when reviewing films, oftentimes leading to a spark of "Oh, yeah! I forgot about that film!"

Movie Ideas for Adult Film Programs

Animation for Adults

The Triplets of Belleville (2003; Columbia TriStar, PG-13)
A Scanner Darkly (2006; Warner Home Video, R)
Persepolis (2007; Sony Pictures, PG-13)
Waltz with Bashir (2008; Sony Pictures, R)

Classic Sci-Fi

Metropolis (1927; Kino, NR)
2001: A Space Odyssey (1968; Warner Home Video, G)
Alien (1979; 20th Century Fox, R)
Blade Runner (1982; Warner Home Video, R)

Comedy Gems

The Apartment (1960; MGM, NR)
Airplane! (1980; Paramount, PG)
Bull Durham (1988; MGM, R)
Kiss Kiss Bang Bang (2005; Warner Home Video, R)

Film Noir

Laura (1944; 20th Century Fox, NR)
Double Indemnity (1944; Universal, NR)
The Big Sleep (1946; Warner Home Video, NR)
The Third Man (1949; Lionsgate, NR)

Great Directors of the 1980s

Martin Scorsese—*Raging Bull* (1980; MGM, R)
Lawrence Kasdan—*Body Heat* (1981; Warner Home Video, R)

Rob Reiner—*This Is Spinal Tap* (1984; MGM, R)

Spike Lee—*Do the Right Thing* (1989; Criterion, R)

Great Directors of the 1990s

Steven Spielberg—*Schindler's List* (1993; Amblin Entertainment, R)

Quentin Tarantino—*Pulp Fiction* (1994; Miramax, R)

James Cameron—*Titanic* (1997; Paramount, PG-13)

The Coen Brothers—*The Big Lebowski* (1998; Focus Features, R)

Love Means Never Having to Say You're Sorry

Casablanca (1942; Warner Home Video, PG)

Love Story (1970; Paramount, PG)

Brokeback Mountain (2005; Focus Features, R)

The Painted Veil (2006; Warner Home Video, PG-13)

Originals and Remakes

Maltese Falcon (1931 & 1941; both films are available on a single MGM Special Edition DVD)

Scarface (1932; Universal, PG; and 1983; Universal, R)

High Noon (1952; Olive Films, NR) and *Outland* (1981; Warner Home Video, R)

Yojimbo (1961; Criterion, NR) and *A Fistful of Dollars* (1964; MGM, R)

Shakespeare Revisited

Forbidden Planet (1956; Warner Home Video, G), based on *The Tempest*

West Side Story (1961; 20th Century Fox, NR), based on *Romeo and Juliet*

Rosencrantz & Guildenstern Are Dead (1990; Image Entertainment, PG), based on *Hamlet*

Scotland, PA (2001; Arts Alliance, R) based on *Macbeth*

War Is Hell

The Bridge on the River Kwai (1957; Sony, PG)

Apocalypse Now (1979; Lions Gate, R)

Inglourious Basterds (2009; Universal, R)

Restrepo (2010; Virgil Films, R)

We Are Not Afraid of Foreign Films!

Rashomon (1950; Criterion, NR)

Rififi (1955; Criterion, NR)

Fanny & Alexander (1982; Criterion, NR)

Crouching Tiger, Hidden Dragon (2000; Columbia TriStar, PG-13)

Woulda Shoulda Coulda (Amazing Films That Lost the Academy Award)

Citizen Kane (1941; Warner Home Video, NR), lost to *How Green Was My Valley*

Raiders of the Lost Ark (1981; LucasFilm, PG), lost to *Chariots of Fire*

GoodFellas (1990; Warner Home Video, R), lost to *Dances with Wolves*

Fargo (1996; MGM, R), lost to *The English Patient*

In addition to these ideas, appendix C offers a list of films inspired by classic works of literature.

Film Programs for Seniors

Seniors can be a very appreciative audience for film programs. Choosing films for seniors can, in the strange way that the world often works, lead to similar problems as finding good movies for teens. Searching for *"films for seniors"* often leads to two kinds of results, either classic films or films featuring plucky seniors such as *Driving Miss Daisy* or *Cocoon*.

There is nothing at all wrong with classics or films featuring plucky seniors, but it's a mistake to think that these are the only sorts of films seniors will be interested in. It can also be easy to overlook (similar to the example I discussed earlier, teen films from the '80s) that seniors are an ever evolving and expanding group. You can't necessarily just throw a black-and-white film up on the screen and call it good.

Your patrons who are in their 70s today were in their 20s and 30s in the '60s and '70s. That means that the directors they may have loved in their heyday weren't William Wyler or Howard Hawks. They were Woody Allen, Mike Nichols, and Francis Ford Coppola. I'm not saying that your

PROGRAMMING TIP
Partner with the Arts!

Events going on in your area are a double source of inspiration for film programming. They can both inspire film program ideas and even serve as opportunities for partnering with other organizations in the area.

What concerts is the symphony doing this year? There are dozens of films and documentaries about musicians, and chances are you can find a film or films about some of the composers the symphony will be performing. The same goes for the art museum. Artists, like musicians, have been inspiring films for years. Museum exhibits can be a great chance to pull out wonderful related history or artist documentaries for programs.

Zoos. Local theaters. Local concerts. Arts festivals. Any of these can potentially provide inspiration for a film program. If you can coordinate your program with the organization, even better—and it creates a wonderful opportunity for both organizations to promote each other.

senior group would love a *Godfather* film program, but one shouldn't rule it out of hand.

If you have a regular group of seniors for whom you design programs, talking to them about what they like is going to be step one. Seniors can be a very appreciative audience for documentaries. My own granny, who just turned 95, told me recently—sounding rather apologetic—"Fiction just doesn't hold my attention anymore. I only have time to learn about 'real' things."

One thing that is crucial for successful programming—for all patrons, but particularly for seniors—is making sure that you have good speakers at a good volume. Frustration at not being able to hear is a fast way to make your seniors unhappy. I also strongly recommend if you're organizing a film program for seniors to consider using closed captioning and to position the film on screen so that it's clearly visible.

Although I think it's best that you have staff present during any film program, I think it's particularly important during any senior film program. The arguments over how to fix the closed captioning during the film programs at my grandparents' senior center are legendary and tales oft repeated. If you or another library staff person is present, you will be immediately available to fix any problem.

In the end, creating a film program is a bit of organization, a bit of planning, a bit of getting to know your audience, and a lot of your own imagination.

Movie Ideas for Senior Film Programs

Great Documentaries

Art, Literature, and Music

F Is for Fake (1976; Homevision, NR)

Genghis Blues (1999; New Video Group, NR)

Mad Hot Ballroom (2005; Paramount, PG)

Wordplay (2006; IFC Films, PG)

Helvetica (2007; Plexifilm, NR)

History, Economics, and Politics

Primary (1960; New Video Group, NR)

The Times of Harvey Milk (1984; Criterion Collection, NR)

500 Nations (1995; Warner Home Video, NR)

The Fog of War (2003; Columbia TriStar, PG-13)

Freakonomics (2010; Magnolia Home Entertainment, PG-13)

People and Places

Salesman (1969; Criterion, NR)

When We Were Kings (1997; Universal, PG)

Good Hair (2009; Lions Gate, PG-13)

Happy (2011; Passion River Films, NR)

Samsara (2011; MPI Home Video, PG-13)

Great Entertainment DVDs

Enjoy the Silence (Great Silent Films)

Robin Hood (1922; Kino, NR)

Sherlock Jr. (1924; Kino, NR)

Battleship Potemkin (1925; Kino, NR)

The Gold Rush (1925; Criterion Collection, NR)

Great Directors of the 1940s and '50s

John Ford—*Grapes of Wrath* (1940; 20th Century Fox, NR)
Howard Hawks—*His Girl Friday* (1940; Columbia TriStar, NR)
Billy Wilder—*Stalag 17* (1953; Paramount, NR)
Alfred Hitchcock—*The Trouble with Harry* (1955; Universal, PG)

Great Directors of the 1960s

David Lean—*Lawrence of Arabia* (1962; Columbia TriStar, PG)
Blake Edwards—*The Pink Panther* (1964; MGM, NR)
Mike Nichols—*The Graduate* (1967; MGM, PG)
George Roy Hill—*Butch Cassidy and the Sundance Kid* (1969; 20th Century Fox, PG)

Great Directors of the 1970s

William Friedkin—*The French Connection* (1971; 20th Century Fox, R)
Mel Brooks—*Blazing Saddles* (1974; Warner Home Video, R)
Francis Ford Coppola—*The Conversation* (1974; Lions Gate, PG)
Woody Allen—*Annie Hall* (1977; MGM, PG)

Intrepid Seniors

Young at Heart (2007; 20th Century Fox, PG)
Beginners (2010; Focus Features, R)
Red (2010; Summit Entertainment, PG-13)
The Best Exotic Marigold Hotel (2011; 20th Century Fox, PG-13)

A Little Less Conversation, a Little More Action (Elvis Movies!)

Jailhouse Rock (1957; Warner Home Video, NR)
G.I. Blues (1960; Paramount, PG)
Girl Happy (1965; Warner Home Video, NR)
Speedway (1968; Warner Home Video, G)

Musicals!

Seven Brides for Seven Brothers (1954; Warner Home Video, G)
Guys and Dolls (1955; Warner Bros, NR)
Fiddler on the Roof (1971; MGM, G)
Cabaret (1972; Warner Bros, PG)

The Rat Pack (Films Starring Some or All of "The Rat Pack")

Rio Bravo (1959; Warner Home Video, NR)—Dean Martin

Ocean's 11 (1960; Warner Home Video, NR)—The Whole Gang

Von Ryan's Express (1965; 20th Century Fox, PG)—Frank Sinatra

Cannonball Run (1981; HBO, PG)—Sammy Davis Jr.

PROGRAMMING TIP
Seek Out What Your Seniors Are Seeking!

Coordinate film showings with new or preexisting programs: Does your library have a quilt show every year? Do you host a regular gardeners group or investment club? There are films about quilting, gardening, and investing, and you may have an easy program with a built-in audience.

Notes

1. American Academy of Pediatrics, "Recommendation on Media Education," *Pediatrics: Official Journal of the American Academy of Pediatrics*, accessed January 7, 2013, http://pediatrics.aappublications.org/content/104/2/341.full; Kyla Boyse, RN, "Television and Children," *University of Michigan Health System*, last updated August 2010, www.med.umich.edu/yourchild/topics/tv.htm#brain.
2. Padma Ravichandran and Brandel France de Bravo, "Young Children and Screen Time (Television, DVDs, Computers)," *National Research Center for Women & Families*, last updated June 2010, www.center4research .org/2010/05/young-children-and-screen-time-television-dvds-computer.
3. *Wikipedia*, sv "BFI List of the 50 Films You Should See by the Age of 14," accessed January 7, 2013, http://en.wikipedia.org/wiki/BFI_list_of_the_50 _films_you_should_see_by_the_age_of_14.
4. Thomas S. Hibbs, "Juvenile List: What Should the Kids Be Watching?" *National Review Online*, December 29, 2005, www.nationalreview.com/ articles/216373/juvenile-list-thomas-s-hibbs.
5. "Fabulous Films," Young Adult Library Services Association (YALSA), accessed January 19, 2012, www.ala.org/yalsa/fabulous-films.
6. Roger Ebert, introduction to *The Great Movies*, NY: Broadway Books, 2002, xv–xvii.
7. Pauline Kael, *Kiss Kiss Bang Bang*, Toronto: Bantam, 1968, 214–215.
8. John Ivan Simon, *John Simon on Film: Criticism 1982–2001*, New York: Applause Theatre & Cinema Books, 2005, 63.

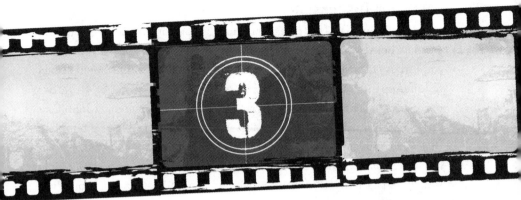

FILM DISCUSSION GROUPS AND SPECIAL PROGRAMS

Once you get the hang of it, film programs are pretty simple. Put the movie in, put out some chairs, and sit at the back to make sure nothing goes wrong. But you may decide you want to up the challenge a bit, or you may be called to incorporate film programming into a larger system program. Do not panic. I have some advice for you here.

Film discussion groups are a natural extension of film and library programming. Film discussion groups are both like and not like book discussion groups. Both require you to do some additional preparation beforehand. Both require you to gather a group of interested participants, since both succeed best with an active group of regulars who enjoy participating.

But film discussion groups require a bit more time investment than book discussion groups. Book discussion groups usually involve the participants reading the book ahead of time. Film discussion groups usually involve the group watching the film together and then discussing it. This makes film discussion groups more of a time commitment both for you and the participants.

Leading a Discussion

Once you have picked the films you want to show for the discussion group, do some homework. Gather information about the film ahead of time that you can use to open the discussion and spark conversation when it seems to lull. Appendix E is a template that recommends information to gather in advance of your discussion. It's based on a handout created by John Fossett for staff at Kitsap Regional Library. Here's an example of a template that I've completed as an example. Please note that if you've never seen the film *Stalag 17*, there are "spoilers" in this film group discussion guide. Resources I used to research this movie include: IMDB, Allmovie.com, Wikipedia, IBDB (the Internet Broadway Database), Amazon.com, TCM.com (Turner Classic Movies), and sensesofcinema.com (Senses of Cinema).

Stalag 17 (1953) Paramount Pictures, Not Rated, 120 minutes

Director
Billy Wilder

Principal Actors
William Holden, Don Taylor, and Otto Preminger

Tagline
"Hilarious, heart-tugging! You'll laugh . . . you'll cry . . . you'll cheer William Holden in his great Academy Award role!"[1] (Reissued print ad)

Source
Adapted from the Broadway play by Donald Bevan and Edmund Trzcinski, which ran for 472 performances from May 8, 1951 to Jun 21, 1952

Awards
Academy Awards: 1954 Best Actor in a Leading Role—William Holden
National Board of Review: NBR Award—Top Ten Films

Nominations
Academy Awards: 1954 Best Actor in a Supporting Role—Robert Strauss; 1954 Best Director—Billy Wilder

Directors Guild of America: 1954 DGA Award: Outstanding Directorial Achievement in Motion Pictures—Billy Wilder

Writers Guild of America: 1954 WGA Award: Best Written American Comedy—Billy Wilder and Edwin Blum

Production Details: February–March 1952; John Show Ranch, Woodland Hills, Los Angeles, CA

Box Office

Budget: $1,661,530 est.; gross: $10,000,000

Trivia

- The film was adapted by Billy Wilder and Edwin Blum, from the play by Bevan and Trzcinski, both of whom were prisoners in Stalag 17 in Austria. Wilder and Blum rewrote the play extensively.[2]
- Playwright Edmund Trzcinski has a cameo as a POW who receives a Dear John letter.
- The movie scenes were filmed in the same order they are shown, a rare occurrence in moviemaking. Many cast members were surprised by the ending.
- A Paramount studio executive requested that Wilder make the prison guards Polish in order to improve the chance of commercial success in West Germany. Wilder, whose mother and stepfather died in concentration camps, was furious and demanded an apology from the executive, who refused. This, along with a disagreement over Wilder's share of the profits from *Stalag 17*, led to the end of Wilder's relationship with Paramount.[3]
- The authors of *Stalag 17* sued CBS and the creators of the TV series *Hogan's Heroes* for plagiarism and received an undisclosed settlement.[4]
- Because of strict time limits, upon receiving the Oscar, William Holden delivered the shortest acceptance speech in Academy Award history up until that time: "Thank you." Holden later took out ads in Hollywood trade publications to thank everyone he wanted to.[5]
- Charlton Heston and Kirk Douglas both turned down the role of Sgt. Sefton because they felt the character was too cynical and selfish. Holden also had reservations but, as he was under contract with

Paramount and "owed them" a film, he was forced to do the movie by the studio.[6]

- The story takes place in December 1944 during the Battle of the Bulge.[7]
- *Stalag 17* was the second pairing of Billy Wilder and William Holden. The first was 1950's *Sunset Blvd.*
- Director Billy Wilder wrote five of the American Film Institute's "100 Funniest Movies": *Some Like It Hot* (#1), *The Apartment* (#20), *The Seven Year Itch* (#51), *Ninotchka* (#52), and *Ball of Fire* (#92).[8]

Themes

- Although not a traditional film noir, *Stalag 17* includes many elements of the genre, including a nihilistic cynical antihero, Sgt Sefton: "Listen stupe. The first week I was in this joint, somebody stole my Red Cross package, my blanket and my left shoe. Well since then I've wised up. This ain't no Salvation Army—this is everybody for himself, dog eat dog."[9]
- During the time *Stalag 17* was made, McCarthyism was rampant in the US. Many people in Hollywood were suffering from the McCarthy blacklist. Some have noted a parallel between the scapegoating of Sgt. Sefton and McCarthyism. What do you think about this? The "real" bad guy turns out to be the head of security. In a time when the government, which is supposed to keep people safe, was seen as a threat by many, do you see this as a relevant detail?[10]
- Some have argued that the story of *Stalag 17* mirrors the story of German prejudice and oppression against Jews and minorities, except Americans are in the role of the Germans. As Americans' freedoms and powers are taken away, they find an "outsider" to ostracize and punish. What do you think about this parallel?[11]
- Wilder uses dark comedy to look at challenging issues of "man's inhumanity to man" in difficult circumstances. Talk about the use of comedy in *Stalag 17*. Does it help communicate some of the deeper themes or obscure them?

Similar Films

- *The Bridge on the River Kwai* (1957), starring William Holden, Alec Guinness, and Jack Hawkins
- *The Great Escape* (1963), starring Steve McQueen, James Garner, and Richard Attenborough

- *The Dirty Dozen* (1967), starring Lee Marvin, Ernest Borgnine, and Charles Bronson
- *Where Eagles Dare* (1968), starring Richard Burton, Clint Eastwood, and Mary Ure
- *Full Metal Jacket* (1987), starring Matthew Modine, R. Lee Ermey, and Vincent D'Onofrio

Ideally you will watch the film before your film discussion group, but even if you don't have time to watch the whole film beforehand, be prepared to watch and take notes during the screening.

There are three main areas to consider when analyzing a film: literary, technical, and dramatic. **Literary analysis** looks at the story and how it is told. Describe the *plot*, which is not to say give a point-by-point "and then" description, but describe the plot's structure. Is it straightforward? Complex? Is it told chronologically (also called *linearly*) or is it in flashbacks, or flash forwards? (Some examples of nonlinear films are *Citizen Kane*, *Rashomon*, and *Momento*.) Is the plot structured or chaotic? Is it fantastical? Is the story resolved or unresolved at the end?

What was the *dialogue* like? Do people really speak that way? If not, is the dialog poetic or have other artistic purpose? (Some examples of films that use artistic dialog: Shakespearean films, the works of Quentin Tarantino.) Did you notice a *theme* or *symbols* in the film? What is the film's *point of view*? What perspective is the story told from? Is there a first person narrator or is it told from a neutral observer's perspective? Is the narrator reliable?

Technical analysis has to do with the process of filming. What is the *cinematography* like? Are there noticeable uses of camera angles, stationary and moving camera, lighting, or special visual effects? What did you notice about the *editing* of the film? Were there noticeably long or short takes? Were there smooth transitions or jump cuts? How was *sound* used in the film? Did the soundtrack enhance, detract, or was it a neutral part of the experience? Were the sound effects realistic? Were they necessary? What about *special effects*? Were they noticeable? Were they necessary?

Dramatic analysis focuses on the acting and setting of the film. Who are the *characters*? What are their strengths and weaknesses? Are the characters believable? Are the *actors* effective in their roles? Do you believe they have captured their characters? Are they appropriately cast? Consider the sets, makeup, costumes, and other elements of the set design. Does the setting work?

PROGRAMMING TIP
Use Your Research to Guide, Not Lecture

John Fossett has led a successful film discussion group for many years. He recommends beginning the discussion with reading the trivia, which his groups always enjoy. Then begin the discussion with as simple a question as "What did you like about the movie?" and "What didn't you like about the movie?" The point of gathering information about the film ahead of time and taking notes during the film is not actually to show that you are the smartest of smarty-pants (which you are, of course!) but to give you the tools to help guide the conversation. Your close analysis provides useful kick-starters if the conversation isn't starting, is starting to lag, or is getting off track.

Gathering Your Film Discussion Group

Gathering a film discussion group may take a bit more work than the advertising you do for a basic film program. Take advantage of any natural audiences for a film discussion group you may have in your area by reaching out to local high schools or colleges. Deliver flyers to local coffee and comic book shops. John Fossett works with a local high school film teacher who has made the Kitsap Regional Library's film discussion group part of his curriculum. Students are required to attend a certain number of the film screenings, but many students have exceeded their required attendance and become regular attendees.

Pick the dates and films for your discussion group ahead of time. Schedule meeting dates for the group at a consistent time and make the upcoming titles known.

Special Programs

Film programs are generally self-contained programs that don't need a lot of hoopla, but you may find an opportunity to integrate film programming into a larger multifaceted program. In this section I will talk about my experience integrating a film programming element into the much larger annual Pierce County Reads program.

Since 2008, the Pierce County Library System (PCLS) has done an annual Pierce County Reads program, an "everyone reads the same book" program held each year in the spring. The program involves a month of programs relating to the book chosen for the year at every branch, culminating with a large event featuring the book's author. Programs at the branches include music, storytelling, cooking, crafting, and community discussion groups related to the book's theme.

PROGRAMMING TIP
Promote Your Group with a Bookmark

Create a bookmark that lists the dates and titles of upcoming discussions, and have plenty on hand during your film program. They're easy to hand out and easy to take home and post on the fridge.

Soon after PCLS began the program, I was asked every year to come up with a "recommended viewing" list of films related to the annual book. Some years it has been easier than others, depending on the theme of the book, but I admit to struggling sometimes to find good films and documentaries that match the book's theme every year. The year of *Three Cups of Tea* was quite difficult as I recall, as was the year of *The Hotel of Bitter and Sweet*. Both years I could find some good documentaries relating the subjects, but little in the realm of well-reviewed entertainment films that fit the theme of the books.

The book for spring 2013 was *The Paris Wife*, a book about Ernest Hemingway's first wife, Hadley, and the couple's early years in Paris. In addition to being asked to come up with a "recommended viewing" list, I was also asked to help the Pierce County Reads committee develop a film programming element that would be part of the many programs available at our various branches. Although I was excited about the film programming element, I confess that once again, I found myself initially stumped coming up with a good list. Yes, there are some movies about Paris in the 1920s, although not as many as you think. There are a few movies featuring Hemingway—although, again, not as many as you think. There are no movies about Hadley. I could come up with a list of Hemingway novels adapted to film, but really, this book is Hadley's story, not Ernest's.

Then I had an epiphany, which seems obvious from the other side. My problem was I was making my focus entirely too narrow. The point, really, is to come up with titles that are related to the themes of the book in question, not match them lockstep. So, what are the themes for *The Paris Wife*? Ernest Hemingway. The 1920s and '30s. Husbands and wives. Paris. I did not need to find films that were about all these things together. I just needed to find films that were about these things. Having this realization broke things open. Here is the recommendation list I came up with for *The Paris Wife*.

Movies Based on Works by Hemingway

A Farewell to Arms (1932; Kino Classics, NR)

Helen Hayes and Gary Cooper star in the tale of love between an ambulance driver and a nurse during World War I. Remade in 1957, starring Rock Hudson and Jennifer Jones.

For Whom the Bell Tolls (1943; Universal, NR)

Gary Cooper and Ingrid Bergman star in the cinematic adaptation of Hemingway's tale of love in the shadow of the Spanish Civil War.

The Sun Also Rises (1957; 20th Century Fox, NR)

Tyrone Power and Ava Gardner star in this story of hard-drinking, hard-partying American expatriates who struggle to find meaning in post-war Europe.

To Have and Have Not (1944; Warner Home Video, NR)

Humphrey Bogart and Lauren Bacall star in this tale of a charter boat operator who gets mixed up with French Resistance fighters and, of course, a dame.

Movies from and about the 1920s and 1930s

Any Human Heart (2011; PBS, NR)

BBC miniseries about a writer whose life intersects with famous and infamous people and events of the twentieth century. He crosses paths with everyone from Ernest Hemingway and Ian Fleming to the Duke and Duchess of Windsor, as he navigates wars and social upheaval.

The Artist (2011; Sony Pictures Home Entertainment, PG-13)

The Best Picture Oscar winner for 2011, this gorgeous movie—about a silent film star on his way out and the beautiful young ingenue on her way up—defied all convention for a best picture winner: it's in black and white and it's a silent film with subtitles. It's also wonderful.

Duck Soup (1933; Universal, NR)

The indomitable Marx Brothers star in this comedy classic wherein Groucho is named the dictator of Freedonia and declares war on neighboring Sylvania for the love of the wealthy Mrs. Teasdale.

The Great Gatsby (1974; Paramount, PG)

Hemingway's contemporary, F. Scott Fitzgerald, also struggled to find meaning in a post-war world, no more so than in the classic *The Great Gatsby*. Robert Redford and Mia Farrow star in the 1974 version of the star-crossed lovers Daisy and Jay. It was remade in 2000 starring Mira Sorvino and Toby Stevens, and a new theatrical version was released in 2013 with Leonardo DiCaprio and Carey Mulligan.

The Kid (1921; American Pop Classics, NR)

Charlie Chaplin's first full-length feature film is also known as being the first "comedy-drama." The melodramatic tale of the tramp rescuing a young orphan promises on its opening screen to be "a picture with a smile and perhaps a tear."

Modern Times (1936; Criterion Collection, NR)

When his boss demands more speed and efficiency, Chaplin goes crazy from his repetitious assembly-line job. With unforgettable gags and sly commentary on class struggle during the Great Depression, it's a timeless showcase of Chaplin's untouchable genius as a director of silent comedy.

A Night at the Opera (1935; Warner Home Video, NR)

The Marx Brothers insinuate themselves into the lives of two opera singers to help them achieve love and success. And laughs! Lots and lots of laughs!

Singin' in the Rain (1952; Warner Home Video, G)

Gene Kelly, Donald O'Connor, and Debbie Reynolds sing and dance their way through this delightful movie about a silent-film production company attempting the difficult transition into talking pictures.

Three Comrades (1938; Warner Bros., NR)

F. Scott Fitzgerald wrote the screenplay of this drama about three young veterans of World War I who all love the same woman.

War Horse (2011; Touchstone, PG-13)

The story of Joey, a British calvary horse during World War I, and Albert, his former owner who enlists to find his beloved horse.

The Women (1939; Warner Home Video, NR)

Partially written by F. Scott Fitzgerald, this classic MGM comedy-drama about the interconnected lives and loves of a group of wealthy socialites stars Norma Shearer, Joan Crawford, and Rosalind Russell.

Movies about Artists and the Women Who Love Them

Pollock (2000; Columbia TriStar, R)

Ed Harris and Marcia Gay Harden star as Jackson Pollock and his wife and helpmeet Lee Krasner. With Krasner's help and encouragement,

Pollock is able to control his drinking and create some of the best work of his career, but his demons are always nipping at his heels.

Surviving Picasso (1996; **Warner Home Video, R**)

Anthony Hopkins stars as Picasso in this Merchant Ivory film about his relationship with Françoise Gilot, a young painter who becomes his lover, his muse, and the mother of two of his children.

Movies about Paris

Amelie (2001; **Miramax, R**)

The gorgeous and delightful film about Amelie, a sweet girl who spreads happiness to the needy and the occasional rough justice to those who deserve it, and her attempt to discover her own true love.

French Kiss (1995; **20th Century Fox, PG-13**)

Kate is a neurotic, phobic American racing to France to try and win her fiancé back from the French goddess who has stolen his heart. Luc is a diamond smuggler who chooses Kate's backpack as a good place to hide his goods. They could not be more different, or hate each other more, or be more perfect for one another!

Hugo (2011; **Paramount, PG**)

Based on the book *The Invention of Hugo Cabret* and directed by Martin Scorsese, this film tells the story of young orphan Hugo Cabret, who lives in the secret hiding holes of a train station in 1930s Paris. Using the skills he learned from his father, a watchmaker, Hugo attempts to repair the only thing his father left him: a fantastical automaton.

Midnight in Paris (2011; **Sony Pictures Classics, PG-13**)

Woody Allen's comedy about a frustrated screenwriter on a trip to Paris who mysteriously finds himself being transported back to the 1920s every night, hobnobbing with the likes of Ernest Hemingway and Gertrude Stein and finding his modern life less and less exciting.

Moulin Rouge (2003; **20th Century Fox, PG-13**)

Satine is the dazzling star of the most infamous nightclub in Paris. Christian is the starving writer who loves her. Zidler is the sadistic ringmaster of the Moulin Rouge who wants to sell Sabine to the sadistic Duke of Worcester. Baz Luhrmann is the director who throws every style and era of entertainment—from Paris cabaret to modern rock to Bollywood to Puccini's *La Bohème*—into the blender and onto the screen for your amusement.

Ratatouille (2007; Disney, G)

With dreams of becoming a world-famous chef, Remy runs away to Paris. The only drawback to realizing his dream? Remy is a rat. Despite the disapproval of his garbage-loving family—and an uncaring world that frowns upon rats in the kitchen—Remy strives to make his dreams come true!

The Triplets of Belleville (2003; Columbia TriStar, PG-13)

A gorgeous, kooky, and thoroughly original animated film about a grandmère searching for her grandson, the preeminent bicycle racer in the world, who has been kidnapped. In desperation, she turns to the Triplets of Belleville, once music stars of Paris in the '30s, now a formidable force against kidnappers and frogs alike.

After coming up with the list of film recommendations, I worked with Tami Masenhimer, a member of the PC Reads committee, to come up with a film programming plan for the branches. We picked seven titles from the list and created Film Discussion Group kits. These kits are available for branches to reserve during the month of PC Reads. Each kit contains a copy of the movie on DVD, a list of guidelines for leading a film discussion group, and a list of questions relating to the particular film to help start the conversation.

The titles we picked to convert into Film Discussion Group kits were:

A Farewell to Arms (1932)
For Whom the Bell Tolls (1943)
Midnight in Paris (2011)
Modern Times (1936)
A Night at the Opera (1935)
Ratatouille (2007)
The Sun Also Rises (1957)

Before PC Reads began, Tami and I met with branch supervisors to go over the basics of leading a film discussion group and gave them discussion guides. An example of the discussion guides can be found in appendixes E and F.

Notes

1. *IMDB*, sv "*Stalag 17*," accessed January 18, 2013, www.imdb.com/title/tt0046359.

2. *Wikipedia*, sv "*Stalag 17*," accessed January 18, 2013, *Wikipedia* http://en.wikipedia.org/wiki/Stalag_17.

3. *IMDB*, sv "*Stalag 17*: Trivia," accessed January 18, 2013, www.imdb.com/title/tt0046359/trivia?ref_=tt_ql_2.

4. Ibid.

5. Ibid.

6. Ibid.

7. Ibid.

8. "AFI's 100 Years . . . 100 Laughs," AFI.com, June 14, 2000, www.afi.com/100Years/laughs.aspx.

9. *IMDB*, sv "*Stalag 17*: Quotes," accessed January 18, 2013, www.imdb.com/title/tt0046359/quotes.

10. Sander Lee, "Scapegoating, the Holocaust and McCarthyism in Billy Wilder's *Stalag 17*," Senses of Cinema, April 4, 2000, http://sensesofcinema.com/2000/feature-articles/stalag.

11. Ibid.

VIEWERS' ADVISORY

I n addition to film programs there is your normal daily interaction with patrons who would like help finding things, including movies. Readers' advisory is of course considered an essential part of library work, but viewers' advisory—helping patrons find that one movie that fits the bill—is often overlooked as a very useful tool.

In my experience, library staff is far more comfortable recommending books to people than they are movies. Sometimes there is even a belief that only a movie "expert" should recommend film titles to people. Perhaps your system has even chosen your "film expert," and you cheerfully funnel all film related questions to that person. This is great for you if the person is there. It may not be so great for that person. Imagine if every book question that ever arose at the library got sent to one person and you start to get a sense of how off this practice is.

What am I saying? You're not confident about your knowledge of films. Yes, you've seen movies, but only the ones you wanted to see. You haven't *studied* them or anything. There are some kinds of movies you don't watch at all. You don't know everything out there! How can you recommend something to someone if you don't know everything that's out there? Well, I am about to reveal a giant secret to you: viewers' advisory is exactly the same as readers' advisory.

Except for our most devoted patrons, no one believes, or even expects, that you have read every book. You don't need to read every book to know how to recommend books to readers. You can even recommend books to readers that you yourself haven't read. You know this is true, and you're comfortable with it. You know about plenty of books that you haven't read. You see them pass on shelving carts; maybe pick some up and scan the jackets. You scan book review columns. You keep track of the best-seller lists.

You also read—mostly what you like, I hope. You do not find it necessary to read things you don't like on the off chance you might have to recommend it to someone. I for one am not a fan of horror, in book or film, but I'm familiar with Steven King, Clive Barker, Thomas Harris, and Dean Koontz even if I don't read much of them, and I even have my backup horror recommendation of T. C. Boyle, who isn't really a horror writer but once wrote a short story collection that scared me so badly I had to stop reading it.

Viewers' advisory is the same, I promise. Every movie and TV show that you've ever seen is research, regardless of your motivations for watching them. Did you watch *Happy Gilmore* because you sprained your ankle and couldn't find the remote? Research. Did you spend last weekend babysitting your nephew and watching back-to-back episodes of *Bubble Guppies*? Research. Do you not have cable and the only channel that your TV set gets is the local PBS affiliate when the wind is blowing the right way and the only show you like to watch ever is *Antiques Roadshow*? Research.

Of course, the more you brush up on movies on a regular basis, the more confident you'll be.

For a very easy, very basic grounding in movies, visit the Internet Movie Database (www.imdb.com) a few times a month. On the front page of the IMDB website, you can see a list of the top films at the box office in the current week, a list of films opening in the current week, a list of "Coming Soon" titles that have the most "buzz," and—most important for those of us in the library business—a list of titles being released on DVD and Blu-ray in the current week, which includes not only movies but popular TV shows as well. Add this to your current professional research rota of *Library Journal*, *Publishers Weekly*, and the *New York Times Book Review* and I think you will be surprised at how fast you start to feel more comfortable with your film collection.

But you don't have time to watch all those movies I'm telling you to read up on every month. Obviously not! I don't have time to watch all those movies, and movies are my job. But you can still know about them and recommend them to people without having seen them. I know, it's a dirty secret I'm letting out of the bag here, but there it is. Here's the other dirty secret: you can recommend things you watched and didn't like!

What am I saying? Recommend terrible movies to people because it doesn't matter? No, that's not what I'm saying at all. What I'm saying is that viewers' advisory, like readers' advisory, involves getting a feel for what the patron standing in front of you likes and guiding her to other things they might like. You hated *Happy Gilmore* when you were trapped on the sofa and couldn't find the remote. But the teenager in front of you just told you that *Dodgeball* is his favorite movie and he likes comedies about sports. Do you know of any others? Yes! Yes you do!

It helps to have titles in your back pocket. As a fan of movies, I would recommend watching them constantly and stuffing your pockets full. As a realist who has trouble seeing even all the movies I'm dying to see, I think cheat sheets, even metaphorical ones, are great. So consider this chapter your cheat sheet.

A few years ago I began working with John Fossett to develop film programming for library conferences. We were motivated by the fact that there just weren't many, if any, film-related programs at library conferences, even though our experience working for libraries showed us that films and TV shows were consistently some of the most popular items we carry. The first program we developed was called "Two Thumbs Up: Genres, Directors and Films to Know for Great Reader's Advisory." It's not a very succinct title, but the purpose of the program was and is to create a comfort level with film by sharing titles in a number of different genres.

The titles we picked were intended to be representative of each genre, but we don't claim that they are "the best" or "the essential" and certainly not "the complete." They are the films that jump out to each of us as great examples of each genre. If you have time to watch some or all of these movies, you'll enjoy many of them, I guarantee—although I'm not crazy enough to suggest you'll love all of them. But mostly I would like you to have these for your back pocket, so you feel confident that you do know some good movies, and you *can* help Mrs. Magillicutty find another musical, even though she's sure she's seen all of them and you've never seen one.

Comedy

The Awful Truth (1937;Columbia, NR). Directed by Leo McCarey. Starring Cary Grant, Irene Dunne, and Ralph Bellamy.

> Divorcees trying to find new romances keep awkwardly and hysterically crossing paths.

Some Like It Hot (1959; MGM, NR). Directed by Billy Wilder. Starring Tony Curtis, Jack Lemmon, and Marilyn Monroe.

> Musicians on the run from the mob disguise themselves as women in an all-female jazz band. Complications, one of whom is Marilyn Monroe, ensue.

Soapdish (1991; Paramount, PG-13). Directed by Michael Hoffman. Starring Sally Field, Kevin Kline, Robert Downey Jr., Cathy Moriarty, Elisabeth Shue, Whoopi Goldberg, and Teri Hatcher.

> The ridiculous off-screen antics of the cast of a popular soap opera begin to spill over onto the set. A crazy-talented cast totally enjoying themselves.

Shaun of the Dead (2004; Universal, R). Directed by Edgar Wright. Starring Simon Pegg and Nick Frost.

> Billed as "A Romantic Comedy with Zombies," the tale of a man who just wants to enjoy a pint at the local pub, if it weren't for all these darn zombies.

Kiss Kiss Bang Bang (2005; Warner Brothers, R). Directed by Shane Black. Starring Robert Downey Jr. and Val Kilmer.

> A "comic noir" about an on-the-run burglar who is mistaken for an actor and cast as a burglar. There's also a wisecracking PI, a beautiful dame, and a murder mystery.

Drama

Captains Courageous (1937; Warner Home Video, NR). Directed by Victor Fleming. Starring Spencer Tracy, Freddie Bartholomew, Lionel Barrymore, Melvyn Douglas, and Mickey Rooney.

> Based on the story by Rudyard Kipling, a spoiled brat is rescued by a fishing boat just heading out to sea. Unwilling to miss the season to return him to shore, the crew put him to work.

The Best Years of Our Lives **(1946; Warner Home Video, NR).** Directed by William Wyler. Starring Fredric March, Dana Andrews, Myrna Loy, and Harold Russell.

> One of the first films to deal directly with the problems of veterans trying to return to their lives after World War II.

Touch of Evil **(1958; Universal, NR).** Directed by Orson Welles. Starring Orson Welles, Charlton Heston, and Janet Leigh.

> A narcotics officer and a corrupt police officer investigate a murder in a small border town.

Doctor Zhivago **(1965; Warner Home Video, PG-13).** Directed by David Lean. Starring Omar Sharif, Julie Christie, Alec Guinness, and Rod Steiger.

> The epic tale of a doctor and poet who is caught up in the Bolshevik revolution.

One Flew over the Cuckoo's Nest **(1975; Warner Home Video, R).** Directed by Milos Foreman. Starring Jack Nicholson, Louise Fletcher, Danny DeVito, and Christopher Lloyd.

> The Academy Award–winning film about a con artist who feigns insanity to avoid prison and finds himself facing shock therapy and Nurse Ratched.

GoodFellas **(1990; Warner Home Video, R).** Directed by Martin Scorsese. Starring Ray Liotta, Robert DeNiro, and Joe Pesci.

> The story of the mob from the view of its foot soldiers, Ray Liotta plays a young man eager to become a wise guy, but the toll it takes on his life and family is enormous.

Musicals

42nd Street **(1933; Warner Home Video, NR).** Directed by Lloyd Bacon, with choreography by Busby Berkley. Starring Warner Baxter, Ruby Keeler, BeBe Daniels, and George Brent.

> The prototypical Busby Berkeley musical with kaleidoscopic dance numbers, this film also features one of the most copied plots in cinema: The big show! The star is down! Can the young ingenue replace her at the last minute?

Gigi **(1958; Warner Bros., G).** Directed by Vincente Minnelli. Starring Leslie Caron, Maurice Chevalier, and Louis Jordan.

> A rich, bored Parisian playboy finds himself delighted by his platonic friendship with the boisterous young Gigi, until Gigi's aunt and grandmamma, retired courtesans both, decide Gigi must become his mistress.

Music Man **(1962; Warner Home Video, G).** Directed by Morton DeCosta, with music and book by Meredith Wilson. Starring Robert Preston and Shirley Jones.

There's trouble in River City when a traveling salesman/con man charms everyone in town except the town's skeptical librarian.

Cabaret **(1972; Warner Bros., PG).** Directed by Bob Fosse, with music by Kandor and Ebb. Starring Liza Minnelli, Michael York, and Joel Grey.

Life in Weimar Republic Berlin is exciting; the cabaret is always beautiful; and the shadow of Nazism all too easy to ignore.

Westerns

Stagecoach **(1939; Criterion Collection, NR).** Directed by John Ford. Starring Claire Trevor and John Wayne.

This classic western—with a place on the National Film Registry—tells the tale of a disparate band of stagecoach travelers traveling west under the threat of Indian attack.

High Noon **(1952; Olive Films, NR).** Directed by Fred Zinnemann. Starring Gary Cooper and Grace Kelly.

With no one willing to lend a hand, a town marshal faces down a dangerous foe alone.

The Naked Spur **(1953; Warner Home Video, NR).** Directed by Anthony Mann. Starring Jimmy Stewart, Robert Ryan, Janet Leigh, Millard Mitchell, and Ralph Meeker.

Bounty hunters trying to bring in a captured murderer are soon at each other's throats over the $5,000 bounty.

The Searchers **(1956; Warner Home Video, NR).** Directed by John Ford. Starring John Wayne, Jeffery Hunter, Ward Bond, and Natalie Wood.

On the National Film Registry, this film stars John Wayne, a Civil War veteran, searching for his young niece, who was captured by the Indians who massacred his family.

A Fistful of Dollars **(1964; MGM, R),** *For a Few Dollars More* **(1965; MGM, R),** *The Good, the Bad and the Ugly* **(1966; MGM, R)**

The spaghetti westerns of Sergio Leone. In the mid-1960s, director Leone ushered in a new era of western. Violent, morally ambiguous, and slyly humorous, all starring the strong silent Clint Eastwood as The Man with No Name.

***The Wild Bunch* (1969; Warner Home Video, R).** Directed by Sam Peckinpah. Starring William Holden, Ernest Borgnine, and Ben Johnson.

Aging outlaws being left behind by progress try for one last big score.

***Lonesome Dove* (1989; Genius Productions, NR).** Directed by Simon Wincer. Starring Tommy Lee Jones and Robert Duvall.

Made-for-TV miniseries based on the novel by Larry McMurtry about two former Texas Rangers driving cattle from Texas to Montana.

***Unforgiven* (1992; Warner Home Video, R).** Directed by Clint Eastwood. Starring Clint Eastwood, Morgan Freeman, and Gene Hackman.

A retired gun slinger reluctantly agrees to take one last job.

Science Fiction

***La Voyage dans la Lune* (1902; Star Film, NR).** Directed by Georges Mielies. Starring Georges Mielies. Available on the DVD *Landmarks of Early Film* (1999; Image Entertainment, NR).

Groundbreaking film from the earliest years of cinema about a magical trip to the moon.

***Metropolis* (1927; Kino, NR).** Directed by Fritz Lang, starring Brigitte Helm, Alfred Abel, Gustav Fröhlich, and Rudolf Klein-Rogge.

Visionary film about a futuristic city where the rich and poor are starkly divided.

***The Day the Earth Stood Still* (1951; 20th Century Fox, G).** Directed by Robert Wise. Starring Patricia Neal and Michael Rennie.

An alien visits earth to warn against mankind's violent ways. Klaatu Barada Nikto! (Remade in 2008, but not well).

***Robot Monster* (1953; Image Entertainment, NR).** Directed by Phil Tucker. Starring George Nader, Claudia Barrett, and George Barrows.

A robot monster (played by a man in a gorilla suit and a diving helmet) threatens all of humanity. His only weakness? Beautiful women, of course. An awesome, dreadful, classic sci-fi film, brought to you in 2-D!

***Invasion of the Body Snatchers* (1956; Olive Films, NR).** Directed by Don Siegel. Starring Kevin McCarthy and Dana Wynter.

The pod people are coming! The pod people are here! A small town doctor frantically tries to warn his community that they are one by one being replaced by aliens. (Remade in 1978, and also in 2007 as *The Invasion.*)

***Planet of the Apes* (1968; 20th Century Fox, G).** Directed by Franklin J. Schaffner. Starring Charlton Heston and Roddy McDowell.

> An astronaut crash-lands on a planet where intelligent apes rule and humans are subjugated. (Followed by four sequels from 1971–1974, a 1974 TV series, a 1981 cartoon TV series, a 2001 remake, and a 2011 sequel to the remake.)

***Soylent Green* (1973; Warner Home Video, PG).** Directed by Richard Fleischer. Starring Charlton Heston and Edward G. Robinson.

> In 2022, the world has run out of food, and mankind survives on the mysterious Soylent Green—which, despite its name, is not vegan.

***Serenity* (2005; Universal, PG-13).** Directed by Joss Whedon. Starring Nathan Fillion, Gina Torres, Alan Tudyk, Adam Baldwin, Jewel Staite, Summer Glau, and Chiwetel Ejiofor.

> Space western about the renegade crew of the ship *Serenity*, who find themselves pursued by an assassin who is after a member of their crew. Based on the 2002 TV series *Firefly*.

Films Based on the Works of Philip K. Dick

***Blade Runner* (1982; Warner Home Video, R).** Directed by Ridley Scott. Starring Harrison Ford, Rutger Hauer, Sean Young, and Edward James Olmos.

> The modern sci-fi classic about a detective charged with hunting down human clones called replicants.

***Total Recall* (1990; Artisan, R).** Directed by Paul Verhoeven. Starring Arnold Schwarzenegger, Rachel Ticotin, and Sharon Stone.

> A construction worker who dreams of visiting Mars tries a service that will implant memories, but something goes terribly wrong. Remade pretty well in 2012, starring Colin Farrell.

***Minority Report* (2002; DreamWorks, PG-13).** Directed by Steven Spielberg. Starring Tom Cruise, Max von Sydow, and Samantha Morton.

> In a future where people are arrested before they commit a crime based on the visions of telepaths, the cop in charge of the program suddenly finds himself being arrested for a crime he's sure he will not commit.

***Paycheck* (2003; Paramount, PG-13).** Directed by John Woo. Starring Ben Affleck and Uma Thurman.

> An engineer wakes up with amnesia, and government agents chasing him for something he can't remember.

***A Scanner Darkly* (2006; Warner Home Video, R).** Directed by Richard
Linklater. Starring Keanu Reeves, Robert Downey Jr., and Winona Ryder.
> Animated film about a future where we have "lost" the War on Drugs
> and most people are addicted to the drug Substance D.

***Next* (2007; Paramount, PG-13).** Directed by Lee Tamahori. Starring
Nicholas Cage, Julianne Moore, and Jessica Biel.
> A magician who can see two minutes into the future is pursued by gov-
> ernment agents who want him to help prevent a terrorist attack.

***The Adjustment Bureau* (2011; Universal, PG-13).** Directed by George
Nolfi. Starring Matt Damon and Emily Blunt.
> A young politician unexpectedly falls in love with a dancer and finds
> that he has crossed purposes with the Adjustment Bureau, a mysteri-
> ous organization in charge of the future.

Horror

***Dracula* (1931; Universal, NR).** Directed by Tod Browning. Starring Béla
Lugosi, Helen Chandler, and David Manners.
> The classic adaptation of the Dracula legend about the evil count who
> terrorizes the countryside in his hunt for human blood.

***White Zombie* (1932; Kino, NR).** Directed by Victor Halperin. Starring
Béla Lugosi and Madge Bellamy.
While they are not quite the lurching, rotting man-eating zombies to which
we have become accustomed, a young couple discovers evil and the first
instances of zombies in American cinema in the Haitian mountains.

***Bride of Frankenstein* (1935; Universal, NR).** Directed by James Whale.
Starring Boris Karloff and Colin Clive.
> Doctor Frankenstein must create a mate for his monster.

***The Wolf Man* (1941; Universal, NR).** Directed by George Waggner. Star-
ring Lon Chaney Jr. and Claude Rains.
> Perhaps one of the best movie tellings of the classic story of man meets
> wolf, man gets bitten by wolf, man becomes wolf and gets chased by
> torch-wielding townsfolk.

***Bud Abbott and Lou Costello Meet Frankenstein* (1948; Universal, NR).**
Directed by Charles Barton. Starring Bud Abbott, Lou Costello, Lon Chaney
Jr., and Béla Lugosi.
> The first—and, many would argue, the best—teaming of comedy leg-
> ends Abbott and Costello with Universal's stable of popular monsters.

Psycho **(1960; Universal, R).** Directed by Alfred Hitchcock. Starring Anthony Perkins, Janet Leigh, and Martin Balsam.

> Hitchcock's tour de force visit to the Bates Motel reinvented the horror picture, made serial killers a staple of modern cinema, and made showers a scarier place to be. (Remade to no useful purpose in 1998.)

Night of the Living Dead **(1968; American Pop Classics, NR).** Directed by George Romero. Starring Duane Jones and Judith O'Dea.

George Romero's first and landmark visit to the zombie/slasher flick threw the horror-flick playbook out the window. Released in the pre-MPAA ratings era and with massive amounts of gore and carnage, the film caused massive uproar when it was first released but is now on the National Film Registry.

The Exorcist **(1973; Warner Home Video, R).** Directed by William Friedkin. Starring Ellen Burstyn, Linda Blair, and Max von Sydow.

> Academy Award–winning horror film about two priests battling to save a girl who has been possessed by the devil. Based on the book by William Peter Blatty, which was inspired by actual events.

More Zombie Films

> *28 Days Later* (2003; 20th Century Fox, R)
> *Dead Snow* (2008; IFC Films, NR)
> *Zombieland* (2009; Columbia Pictures, R)
> *Zombies of Mass Destruction* (2009; Lions Gate, R)
> *The Walking Dead* (TV series, 2010–present; Anchor Bay, TV-MA)
> *Warm Bodies* (2013; Summit Entertainment, PG-13)

Hammer Horror

The UK studio Hammer Films is famous for its gothic horror pictures made from the 1950s through 1970s. These films drift in and out of being available. Many are available on the DVD set *TCM Greatest Classic Films Collection: Hammer Horror.*

> *The Curse of Frankenstein* (1957)
> *Dracula* (1958)
> *The Mummy* (1959)

The Revenge of Frankenstein (1959)
The Brides of Dracula (1960)
The Evil of Frankenstein (1964)
Dracula: Prince of Darkness (1966)
Frankenstein Created Woman (1967)
Dracula Has Risen from the Grave (1968)
Taste the Blood of Dracula (1969)
Frankenstein Must Be Destroyed (1969)
The Horror of Frankenstein (1970)
Scars of Dracula (1970)
Dracula AD 1972 (1972)
The Satanic Rites of Dracula (1973)
Frankenstein and the Monster from Hell (1974)
The Legend of the 7 Golden Vampires (1974)

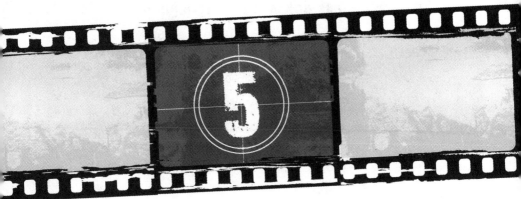

EQUIPMENT

Equipment might be one of the more intimidating aspects of film programming. What kind of equipment do you need? Can your library afford it? Do you know how to use it? What's "the best" choice of projector/player/screen/speakers/setup?

So before you panic, the first thing to know is that good film programming is available on any budget. You need a screen of some kind, something with which to play the film, and decent speakers. This can be a DVD player hooked up to a television screen. This could even be a DVD played on a laptop, depending on the audience and type of film you are showing. Obviously the sky's the limit in how elaborate an audio-visual setup a library can have, but most library systems operate with slightly lower budget limitations than the sky.

The Bare Necessities of Film Programming

SCREEN	PROJECTOR	PLAYER	SOUND
television	LCD projector (portable or mounted)	DVD/Blu-ray player	internal TV or computer speakers
wall-mounted monitor		laptop/computer	detachable speakers
projection screen			amplifier
wall			portable sound system
sheet			mounted sound system

When showing a film, you can either display it or project it. Displaying the film requires a television or monitor. Projecting requires a projector and a screen. There are many who will insist—not without cause—that projection is the best way to show films. Even with the current mania for large screen televisions, a projector can usually get you a bigger image than a monitor. A projected image also most closely resembles the movie theater experience. The more large groups attend your programs, the more you will want to consider projecting rather than displaying your film.

If you do not have means for projecting a film but have a decent-quality television or monitor, you can still definitely do film programs. The most important thing to keep in mind, though, is that the smaller the screen, the smaller the audience will need to be. Nothing sucks the joy out of a film program faster than thirty adults crammed around a 19-inch television screen.

The Visual Experience

Most of the librarians I polled about their film programs who do not have access to an installed projector system use a laptop or DVD player plugged into an LCD projector or into a mounted television screen. Many libraries have meeting rooms with an installed projector and sound system. Many more have portable LCD projectors that can be used for film programming.

Projectors

There are pros and cons to both mounted projectors and portable projectors.

The major pro for a mounted projector is that it's always there. If your system is anything like my system, getting portable equipment for a program can mean reserving it, making sure other staff members can get it to you on time, and, in the worst-case scenario, running all over the system trying to pick one up in time for a program.

A mounted projector is also already set up and ready to go, for the most part. Although I recommend always testing any kind of AV set up before your audience arrives, mounted systems often have less of the necessary fussing over setup that portable systems do.

Another positive to installed projectors is what one librarian I spoke to called their "untheftability." You don't have to worry about them walking away. You also don't have to worry about the kinds of losses that have nothing to do with theft, such as lost cables or the other peripherals that travel with a portable projector but occasionally miss the boat.

But there are drawbacks to mounted projectors, particularly those mounted on the ceiling. Projectors need care and adjusting, and if they are locked up tight or installed in the ceiling, you could be stuck with a picture that needs adjusting and no way to do it without a maintenance request. Projectors need to be cleaned regularly, as anyone who has had to watch a movie with a speck of dust on the lens can attest. You want to be able to get to your projector to do both simple and more complicated adjustments that are a matter of course, preferably without having to use a ladder.

The main benefit of a *portable projector* is flexibility. If you have multiple spaces that can be used to screen films, a portable projector allows you to use them to their full advantage. Portable projectors also allow easy adjustment and cleaning, and more flexibility in positioning than mounted projectors. They're also cost efficient. Assuming things are well scheduled, multiple programs and locations can share projectors.

I've already touched on some of the drawbacks of portable projectors, but they're important to review because many of them can be avoided with careful time and planning. It's vital that when a projector travels, all the cables and power cords go with it. If it has a remote that you need or want to use, it needs to travel too, as well as have an up-to-date battery.

A portable projector also needs a surface to sit on while displaying the film. Invest in a rolling equipment cart if there's no obvious place in the room to set it up. It needs to be somewhere that it can both display the picture and be connected to power. Make sure the cord is long enough to reach the juice. It seems like it would go without saying, but I myself have been caught in programs where I couldn't set the projector up where I wanted because I didn't have a long-enough electrical cord.

Positioning the projector can be challenging, and it can be a drawback of using a portable projector. The ideal location is centered on the screen, as many feet back as needed to get the picture size and quality you want. Unfortunately this often creates a dead space in the center of the room where people can't sit. Depending on the size of the room or crowd, this is not an insurmountable problem, but it's something that needs to be planned for when setting out chairs or seating areas.

TIP
Prevent Distortion

For setting up the projector I asked John Fossett, who has been doing film programming for Kitsap Regional Library for many years, to give us the rundown:

"Take the time to align the projector. Get it as square to the screen and level to the floor as possible. This prevents distortion around the edges of the projection. Make sure your screen is flat with no wrinkles. Screens that lower from the ceiling often have a slight bow when lowered completely. Raising the screen slightly usually will get it to lay flat."

Monitors

The alternative to a projector is, of course, the tried-and-true television screen. I'm not going to spend much time talking about your old-school television connected to a DVD player, because I think they're pretty self-explanatory. However, we are in the middle of a brave new world of flat-screen technology, which offers some exciting options for film programming.

Flat-panel, also referred to as HDTV, monitors—which can be mounted onto the wall—are the wave of the future for all of us, including libraries. The big shift to make when thinking about these screens is that, just as a computer monitor is separate from the computer which data it displays, a flat-panel screen is separate from whatever it is displaying. Flat panels can be connected to a laptop, the Internet, cable, or a DVD/Blu-ray player.

The main kinds of flat panel screens are *CFL* or *LED back-lit LCD* or *plasma*. There are adherents for all of them. All have versions that range in size, quality, and price. Lately there has also been a strong marketing push for 3-D televisions. Because technology evolves so quickly, rather than attempt any detailed discussion of specific brands, I encourage you to check out resources such as *Consumer Reports* and *PC Magazine* to evaluate the latest information on which specific screen might be right for your library. I will, however, offer a general discussion of the different screens.

Plasma screens were the first flat-screens on the market and for a long time were considered the gold standard. The quality of *LCD screens*, particularly with the addition of using LED lighting, has caught up with plasma. As LCD screens have taken over more and more of the market, plasma screen makers are now focusing primarily on the very big screens (70 inches) and 3-D television technology.

Plasma screens are known for being both exceptionally thin and very large. A plasma screen is made up of thousands of gas-filled cells, which are ionized by an electric grid. The ionized cells phosphor or, in exceptionally lay terms, light up the screen. The benefits of plasma screens are:

- film-quality images with excellent color
- high-quality images displayed from high-definition television, Blu-ray, and progressive-scan DVD players
- a wide viewing angle, meaning you can sit to the side rather than directly in front of the screen and still get a good picture

Some of the drawbacks of plasma screens are:

- They are susceptible to burn-in, which is a permanent discoloration of the display caused by an uneven use of the pixels. Due to the burn-in phenomenon, plasma screens are not a good choice for gaming.

- They can suffer from ghosting, which is not the same as burn-in, but similar, where previous images linger on the screen. It can be especially noticeable when a bright image is replaced with a dark image.
- Although plasma screens are famous for amazing color displays, they have traditionally not done well in transmitting true reds, which often display as more orange.
- They have a short life span. The nature of the phosphor based screen is that they lose brightness over time. Most plasma screens have a lifespan of five to six years.

LCD screens have been greatly improved by the introduction of LED backlighting, although LED-backlit LCD screens are still on the more expensive side. Some of the benefits of LCD screens are:

- excellent color display
- dual use as a computer display or gaming display
- limited to no burn-in
- excellent energy efficiency for LED-backlit LCD screens

Some of the drawbacks to LCD screens are:

- They can have a limited viewing angle, although manufacturers have been working hard to improve this. This means that in a big room, people sitting on the side angles of the screen might have a hard time seeing the picture without experiencing distortion.
- They can have a slow pixel-response time, leading to the ghosting effect I mentioned with plasma screens.
- They are not as bright as plasma or traditional television screens, meaning there can be issues with clear viewing in a lit room.

3-D Televisions

Since 3-D screens are being pushed as the next big wave, I feel I should mention them, although it is not to recommend them. Although I specifically wish to refrain from recommending whether your system gets a plasma or LCD screen, there are some inherent problems with the 3-D screen that I think make them a questionable investment for a public library.

All the AV experts I asked about 3-D televisions while researching this chapter made it clear they felt that, despite the push they are getting from the industry, these TVs are essentially gimmicks. The public has certainly responded in a very lukewarm fashion to them, as one can see by the number of them one finds on sale everywhere.

There are lots of issues that make the 3-D television problematic. There are the expensive 3-D glasses you need to buy and use with the set. There's the question of whether having purchased a 3-D set you also wish to invest in a 3-D Blu-ray player, which will allow the set to work at its best. But really the primary drawback to a 3-D television is the lack of content. A quick search of your library's catalog should show you the dearth of 3-D films currently available to make an investment in this technology worthwhile.

Sound

Another common thread emerged when speaking to librarians about the setups they use. They all use some form of detachable speakers. In fact, when I polled library staff about film programming, the one consistent piece of feedback I received across the board is to make sure that you have good speakers.

Speakers can be the Achilles' heel of any film program. It's the one item many people do not consider when setting up a program, and short of projection equipment failure or a skipping or broken disc, poor sound is the one area most likely to cause unhappiness with a program.

The mistake many intrepid film programmers make is believing that the internal speakers within one's laptop or television will be sufficient for a room full of people. Space swallows sound, as do bodies. The other mistake is not making sure that any detachable speakers you use have enough oomph to fill the room. Detachable speakers are almost always better than the internal speakers of a computer or television, but they still vary widely in quality and power.

This brings us to the issue of amplifiers, soundboards, or other portable audio systems. Many a film programmer gets by without the use of one of these, but the fact is a soundboard, a portable PA system, or even audio-tuning software on your PC (provided your PC is attached to some good speakers) is going to allow you to tweak the sound in a way that will maximize the enjoyment of your audience. Anyone who has ever wrestled with speakers knows that often just a volume control is not enough. You may have your speakers turned to the proverbial "11," but if the sound mix is off, you just have a loud, garbled annoyance. You don't need to have the mad skills of a DJ or spend hours tweaking every little sound nuance, but you should be familiar with how to adjust the volume, tone, and balance.

Blu-ray and DVD

As professionals who have seen the rise and fall of many audiovisual formats over the years, librarians could be forgiven for being exhausted at the thought of yet another format war. There are some differences between the current DVD/Blu-ray format competition and those that have come before it. These differences have made the issue both easier and harder for libraries to make the choice about when, or even if, to start carrying Blu-ray.

Blu-ray has not supplanted DVD in the way that DVD so quickly supplanted VHS. As of yet, the movie industry still seems interested in releasing films on both DVD and Blu-ray, although anyone who buys films knows they've also started getting creative with some titles: packaging the DVD and Blu-ray together or occasionally releasing a title only on Blu-ray. The fact that Blu-ray players can play both DVD and Blu-ray has meant we have so far avoided that sudden shift where suddenly all our patrons have DVD players and nothing to play in them. Add the twist of the burgeoning popularity of streaming and downloading video content and you have, at best, an unclear future for film formats.

This book is about film programming and not film collection development, so I'm afraid I'm not going to delve into the question about when, or if, you should bite the bullet and start collecting Blu-ray. Yes, definitely, probably, maybe, sometime is about as far as many of us have gotten.

From a film programming perspective, it's almost universally agreed that Blu-ray provides a superior picture experience than DVD, especially if you're watching the Blu-ray on a screen that is up to Blu-ray quality. If you show films on a plasma or LCD screen, a Blu-ray is going to give you a better picture than a DVD. That said, if you are playing a DVD on an LCD or plasma screen, or with a high-quality LCD projector, the picture quality is not going to suck.

The DVD/Blu-ray picture quality debate does remind me sometimes of the joke about American dentists announcing that our teeth just cannot possibly get any whiter. If the choices are between great and really great, you can be reasonably confident regardless of which one you choose. There will be people reading this who don't agree with me, and I'm sure you have that one patron who will talk your ear off for days about how much superior a Blu-ray is to a DVD, but for your film programming, good-quality equipment and a clean disc are what you need. Whether it is a DVD or a Blu-ray disc, I believe the results will be fine.

Preparing for Your Program

You've picked out your film. You've advertised it, reserved your room, and gathered your audience. You've even made some lovely displays of books and films related to your topic so your audience will have something to check out when they're done with the film. You've set up the chairs and prepared your opening remarks. You've made coffee and put out popcorn and those funny little sugar cookies that no one really likes unless they're the only things available to eat—in which case, *wow*, they're awesome. As much as all this is, if you haven't taken the time to prep your equipment, you are setting yourself up for program failure.

In this particular respect, film programming differs greatly from book programming. With a book program, you can, in fact, walk into the meeting space ten minutes or less before the program starts with no worries. Unless and until you are 100 percent confident with your equipment, how to set it up, how it works, how to troubleshoot issues, you must plan for time to set up your equipment properly.

Here are some very important questions you need to answer when you begin to plan your program, and when I say "begin to plan" I mean "begin to plan," not the day before (or of!) the show.

The Film Itself

Do you have a copy of the film you want to show? Is it clean? Do you need to place a hold on it to have it sent to you? Have you given yourself enough time to evaluate the disc when it comes for quality? Have you given yourself enough time to clean the disc? Do you need the system to purchase a copy for you? If so, have you established with the collection development department how long that process will take? Have you let the collection development department know that you need the film for a program, so that they will deliver it to you rather than send it out into circulation?

Taking the time to make sure that the disc is clean and fully functional is time very well spent. Lots of people use the DVDs in our libraries. Lots of those discs are dirty. A dirty disc can lead to skipping, frozen pictures, or garbled sound. If you are taking a DVD off the shelf to show, cleaning it first is a no-brainer. After it's clean, look it over for any visible scratches or other issues that might signal problems. Watch it, or play it in the background with the sound off if you (like most of us) do not have time to watch a movie in the middle of your day. Make sure it gets through to the end without skips or jumps. Take the time to listen to enough of it to make sure the sound is clear.

Work closely with your collection development department on film programming if they are not already involved. It may be very easy for them to order you a new copy of a title you wish to show, but not if they don't have enough lead time. If for some reason you are showing your own copy, or a nonlibrary copy of a film, let the collection development department know. They may want to make sure it's a title the system has in its collection. No selector wants a phone call from a staff person or patron saying that they saw an amazing film at the library the other day and don't understand why it's not available for checkout. Give your collection development department the opportunity and lead time to support your film programs.

The Equipment Itself

Do you know where it is? If it's something you need to reserve, have you done so? Do you know how to set up all of the equipment without help? Do you know where all the cables and cords attach and what they do? Do you know how to recognize if one of those cables or cords is missing? If you have an installed audiovisual system, do you know how to turn it on and get it working? If it's under lock and key, do you have the key? Do you know how to troubleshoot problems that inevitably arise with any technical setup? Have you tested both video and sound quality? Do you know how to adjust them? Do you know who to call when there are problems? Does that person know that you might be calling them?

The last two questions dealing with whom to call when there are problems are ones that are important, but also ones that can backfire if you consistently rely on your AV expert or IT department to do setup and problem solving for you. Obviously even the most expert film programming librarian may encounter technical problems that are beyond their abilities to solve. But you absolutely want to know as much as you can about how to get your equipment up and running so that if you do have to call in an expert, they're not running over on a Sunday night because you couldn't figure out where the power button is.

The main benefit of doing all this preparation well ahead of time is that it saves you from that horrible panic that inevitably sets in when you have a room full of people waiting for a movie and you've just realized that the bulb is burned out, or the power cord is missing, or even that it's just not working the way it did the last time you did a film program. Discovering problems at the last minute inevitably amplifies the situation, turning something that could be a very simple fix (finding the power cord, or swapping your not-working projector for a working one) into a crisis (calling the IT guy at home on a Sunday evening).

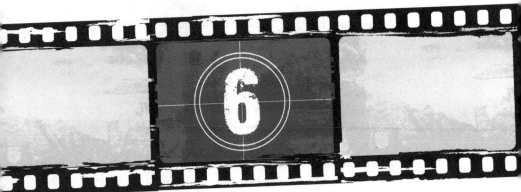

LEGALITIES AND RELATED ISSUES

The most challenging part of film programming—but in many ways the most important—is making sure you are in compliance with the law relating to public screening of films. If developing film programs is the visit to the candy store, the legal part is the trip to the dentist. It's a drag, but it's vital for a successful and long-lived film programming at your library.

DVD/Blu-rays are generally released by the studios with the designation of "Home Use Only." This means exactly what it says: they are intended for the use of an individual or family inside the home. Here is the official word from the MPAA (italics mine):

> The Federal Copyright Act (Title 17 of the US Code) governs how copyrighted materials, such as movies, may be used. Neither the rental nor the purchase of a copy of a copyrighted work carries with it the right to publicly exhibit the work. No additional license is required to privately view a movie or other copyrighted work with a few friends and family or in certain narrowly defined face-to-face teaching activities. However, bars, restaurants, private clubs, prisons, lodges, factories, summer

camps, *public libraries*, daycare facilities, parks and recreation departments, churches, and non-classroom use at schools and universities are all examples of situations where *a public performance license must be obtained.* This legal requirement applies regardless of whether an admission fee is charged, whether the institution or organization is commercial or nonprofit, or whether a federal or state agency is involved.

"Willful" infringement of these rules concerning public performances for commercial or financial gain is a federal crime carrying a maximum sentence of up to five years in jail and/or a $250,000 fine. Even inadvertent infringement is subject to substantial civil damages.[1]

So, there you have it. It's pretty clear. Public showings of films, even by nonprofit or educational organizations, are not allowed unless you have taken the additional step of obtaining a *public performance license*, also referred to as an *umbrella license*, or you can purchase a film that comes with *public performance rights*. The primary difference between public performance rights and a public performance license is that one covers the film itself and the other covers a location.

Public Performance Rights

When they are available, public performance rights (PPR) come with the film when you purchase it. Sometimes the film is offered with two different price points, one for regular viewing and another, higher cost that includes PPR. Public performance rights are usually attached to educational videos, although some entertainment film producers not associated with big studios also offer PPR.

Using films with PPR is a good option for libraries that don't wish to get a site license but would still like to do film programming. It's a good option if you wish to show documentary and other educational films rather than feature films. If you have an umbrella license, you may still find yourself wanting to show a film that is not covered under the umbrella but which may have PPR. Another benefit of purchasing films with public performance rights is that the performance rights are with the film, not the library's location. If a patron wishes to check out the film and show it to their Rotary Club or PTA, or if the library wishes to sponsor an off-site screening in conjunction with a local group, you can do so legally.

There are a few downsides to public performance rights. You are limited to the selection of films that come with PPR, which leans toward documentaries rather than feature films. You generally have to pay more for PPR—occasionally a lot more. In addition to supporting the cost of making expensive documentaries, the high cost also reflects what many producers see as their main audience: schools and universities. It may make perfect sense for a university to shell out a few hundred dollars for a documentary that will be used as part of a curriculum, but it's harder for a public library intending to show it once or twice to justify such an expense.

In answer to this very problem, a new PPR film option has recently been developed. Some educational film producers, such as Bullfrog Films, offer a rental option: you can rent a title from them for a limited time at significantly lower cost than purchasing. The rental includes the right to show the film.[2]

Generally I view one of the benefits of film programming as showcasing what is in the library's collection, which the renting option does not allow you to do. However, if you are doing a larger program on a special subject, it may make perfect sense to rent a film that is a perfect fit with the topic at hand.

This brings me to one of the best benefits of public performance rights. Generally the studios that offer films with PPR are smaller organizations with specialized missions. They produce high-quality work that often cannot be seen anywhere else. They often offer films that are not covered by public performance umbrella licenses, which tend to focus on larger studios. If part of the mission of your film programming is to turn your patrons on to rare gems they may never get another opportunity to see, PPR films can be a wonderful option.

Some PPR Providers

Many of the companies that provide films with public performance rights are focused on educational and curriculum support videos that may not be the best fit for public library showings. Here's a list of companies that offer PPR films that can work well for programming in a public library setting. In many cases the PPR cost is clearly indicated, but in some instances, you will need to contact the company directly to arrange public performance rights.

CHAPTER 6

Ambrose Video Publishing Inc.

28 West 44th Street, Suite 1115
New York, NY 10036
800-526-4663
www.ambrosevideo.com

Focus is documentaries on literature, science, and history appropriate for teen and adult audiences.

Aquarius Health Care Media

30 Forest Road
PO Box 249
Millis, MA 02054
508-376-1245
www.aquariusproductions.com

Focus is health-related documentaries and educational films including (but not limited to) those relating to issues of adolescence, such as bullying and teen health, and aging, such as Alzheimer's and caregiving.

ArtMattan Productions (contact directly about PPR)

535 Cathedral Parkway
Suite 14B
New York, NY 10025
212-864-1760
www.africanfilm.com

Films about the human experience of black people in Africa, the Caribbean, North and South America, and Europe. The films have all been screened as part of the African Diaspora Film Festival.

Bullfrog Films

PO Box 149
Oley, PA 19547
800-543-3764
www.bullfrogfilms.com

Films for children and adults that focus on a wide range of topics, but particularly on the environment and sustainable living. Includes films from the National Film Board of Canada, CBC, Television Trust for the Environ-ment, BBC, and other film producers from around the world.

California Newsreel

500 Third Street, Suite 505
San Francisco, CA 94107–1875
415-284-7800
http://newsreel.org
Focus on films about social justice, globalization, and multiculturalism. Includes the Library of African American Cinema.

Chip Taylor Communications

2 East View Drive
Derry, NH 03038
800-876-CHIP (2447)
http://chiptaylor.com
Educational films for children and adults on subjects "from Art to Zoology." Includes many titles on crafting and art.

Christian Cinema (contact directly about PPR)

130 N. Kelsey St., Suite C
Visalia, CA 93291
888-919-0184
www.christiancinema.com
Features many "Dove Family–Approved" films. Christian Cinema works with MPLC to provide public performance rights.

CinéFête

1586 Fleury East, suite 210
H2C 156
Montreal, QC
Canada
800-858-2183
http://usa.cinefete.ca
Canadian company specializing in multi-language documentaries and

educational films. Many award-winning animated films for children. Large number of French language films.

The Cinema Guild (contact directly about PPR)

115 W. 30th St., Ste 800
New York, NY 10001
800-723-5522
www.cinemaguild.com
Focus on providing award-winning documentaries and independent film to the educational community.

Destination Education

PO Box 6124
Lincoln, NE 68506–0124
402-435-0110
http://shopdei.com/ecommerce/catalog.php
Primarily films for education and curriculum support, but they carry *Reading Rainbow*.

Discovery Education

Customer Service
PO Box 2284
South Burlington, VT 05407–2284
888-892-3484
www.discoveryeducation.com
PPR versions of Discovery Channel, Science Channel, Animal Planet, and Planet Green programs designed for the school market. Includes some perennial public library favorites such as *Myth Busters*, *How It's Made*, and Jeff Corwin and Bill Nye shows.

Disney Educational Productions

105 Terry Drive, Suite 120
Newtown, PA 18940
215-579-8589
http://dep.disney.go.com/
The educational side of Disney, including Disney productions on social studies, history, language and arts, and math and science. Includes the Disney-

nature catalogue as well as popular series such as *ABC News Classroom*, *Bill Nye the Science Guy*, and *Schoolhouse Rock*. Except for the Disneynature films, Disney Educational Productions does not include Disney feature films.

Docurama Films

New Video Group
902 Broadway, FL 9
New York, NY 10010
212-206-8600
www.docurama.com
Features critically acclaimed, cutting-edge, and award-winning documentaries.

Ergo Video (contact directly about PPR)

PO Box 2037
Teaneck, NJ 07666
877–539–4748
www.jewishvideo.com
Films from around the world focusing on the Jewish experience.

Fanlight Productions

c/o Icarus Films
32 Court Street
Brooklyn, NY 11201
800-876-1710
www.fanlight.com/titleindex/title.php
A subsidiary of Icarus Films, Fanlight focuses on documentaries about aging, health care, disabilities, family relationships, social issues, ethics, mental health, and social work.

Film Ideas Inc.

308 North Wolf Rd.
Wheeling, IL 60090
800-475-3456
www.filmideas.com
Includes a wide array of documentaries and series, including extensive collection of travel films.

Film Movement

109 West 27th Street
Suite 9B
New York, NY 10001
212-941-7744 ext. 205
www.filmmovement.com
Film Movement is a unique subscription service that delivers new films from independent cinema every month. Each film comes with a one-time screening license, and also promotional materials such as posters.

Films for the Humanities and Sciences

132 West 31st Street
17th Floor
New York, NY 10001
800-322-8755
http://ffh.films.com
Focus is on films for higher education in the humanities and sciences. Geared toward the classroom, but features some interesting programming gems, including historic old films and newsreels on DVD.

Green Planet Films

PO Box 247
Corte Madera, CA 94976
415-377-5471
http://greenplanetfilms.org/
Nonprofit distributor of nature and environmental films.

Icarus Films

32 Court Street, 21st Floor
Brooklyn, NY 11201
718-488-8900
http://icarusfilms.com
"Distributing innovative and provocative documentaries from independent producers around the world." Icarus offers a rental option for a one-time

screening, which can be significantly less expensive than purchase. Contact Icarus directly with questions about renting.

International Historic Films Inc. (contact directly about PPR)

PO Box 29035
Chicago, IL 60629
773-927-2900
ihffilm.com/info.html
Extensive collection of military history documentaries.

Kino Lorber Education

333 West 39th Street
Suite 503
New York, NY 10018
212-629-6880
www.kinolorberedu.com
Films from Kino International and Lorber Films with public performance rights. Wide selection of classic, independent, and documentary films.

Live Oak Media

PO Box 652
Pine Plains, NY 12567
800-788-1121
www.liveoakmedia.com
Live Oak Media, known for producing picture book read-alongs on CD, also produces picture book DVDs shot directly from the source material and featuring word-for-word narration.

Moving Images Distribution (contact directly about PPR)

103–511 West 14th Avenue
Vancouver BC V5Z 1P5
Canada
800-684-3014
Wide selection of documentary, educational, informational, and animated films for children and adults.

National Geographic Educational

School Publishing
PO Box 11305
Des Moines, IA 50347
800-627-5162
www.nationalgeographic.com/education
Must contact National Geographic directly to inquire about PPR. National Geographic titles bought through third-party vendors do not include PPR.

New Day Films

190 Route 17M
PO Box 1084
Harriman, NY 10926
888-367-9154
www.newday.com
Features documentaries in a wide range of topics, including many that have been nominated for or won Academy Awards, Emmys, and other film honors.

PBS Educational Media

1320 Braddock Place
Alexandria, VA 22314
800-424-7963
http://teacher.shop.pbs.org
Does not include PBS Home Video, although there are PBS Educational Media versions of many popular PBS documentaries and series.

Princeton Book Company (contact directly for PPR)

614 Route 130
Hightstown, New Jersey 08520
www.dancehorizons.com
800-220-7149
Princeton Book Company/Dance Horizons carries dance-related films from a variety of sources, only some of which have PPR. Contact directly for questions about individual titles.

Questar Inc. (contact directly about PPR)

307 N. Michigan Ave., Suite 500
Chicago, IL 60601
800-544-8422
www.questar1.com
Features a wide range of travel, nature, food, entertainment, and family programming.

Rich-Heape Films Inc.

5952 Royal Lane, Suite 254
Dallas, Texas 75230
888-600-2922
www.richheape.com
Films that increase awareness of Native Americans and other native peoples.

Spoken Arts

195 South White Rock Road
Holmes, New York 12531
800-326-4090
www.spokenartsmedia.com
In addition to picture book read-alongs on CD, Spoken Arts features picture books on DVD.

The Video Project

200 Estates Dr.
Ben Lomond, CA 95005
800-4-PLANET (800-475-2638)
www.videoproject.org
Documentaries on the environment, health, and global issues.

Women Make Movies

462 Broadway, Suite 500WS
New York, NY 10013
212-925-0606
www.wmm.com/
Films by and about women.

TIP
Ask and You *May* Receive

If you have a movie that you particularly want to show but it is not from any of
the companies listed above, if it is not covered by an umbrella license (discussed
below), or if your library does not have an umbrella license, you can always try contacting the filmmakers or studio directly. You may not get anywhere—or where you get
may be too expensive to be worthwhile—but it's also possible, especially with smaller
independent studios, that they would be delighted to work with a public library to
arrange a showing.

Public Performance Licenses

Public performance licenses—also called site licenses, umbrella licenses,
or blanket licenses—are purchased for a location. They allow the purchasing organization, be it school, church, or library, to show films at a specific
location. The films that can be shown depend on the license purchased.

There are two main companies that provide site licenses, Movie Licensing USA and MPLC. Each company represents a different set of film producers and studios, with some overlap. With a site license, a library may
show films from any of the studios covered by the license. A library can purchase a license from one of these companies or from both of these companies. Buying a license from both provides access to the largest range of films.

Licenses are location specific, meaning a license must be purchased for
every location at which you would like to show films. If you are a library
system or consortium, you will need to purchase a separate license for each
location where you wish to do film programming. You do not have to buy
licenses for all your branches, but you can show films covered by the license
only at branches that have one.

Pricing of the license depends on the population in your library's service area. As is often the way, the more licenses you are purchasing, the
more certain discounts can be negotiated. Several states have negotiated with
Movie Licensing USA and MPLC to provide licenses to libraries within the
state at reduced rates. When considering whether to get a license, contact
your state library or state library organization to see if you are eligible for
a reduced rate.

> ## TIP
> ### Nimble Negotiating
>
> If your system or consortium has only a few branches that have licenses, it can make sense for the individual branch to deal with the licensing company directly. If, however, you have multiple or all locations covered by licenses, you should strongly consider having one person or department responsible for negotiating price and handling the annual license renewal. This will ensure that you are able to get the best price for your system and standardize the renewal process across the system.

What Does a License Do, Exactly?

The federal guidelines for copyright protection of motion pictures are, as mentioned above, very clear. Showing a movie in a public setting without permission from the studio is a violation of copyright. Now, every time a library wishes to show a film they could, conceivably, contact the studio directly and request permission. The result would probably be frustrating and possibly expensive, since the answer could well be "Sure, that will cost two thousand dollars."

When you purchase a license from MPLC or Movie Licensing USA, you are purchasing pre-negotiated permission from the studios. MPLC and Movie Licensing USA work directly with the studios to hammer out these permissions. When you purchase the license, every studio covered by MPLC or Movie Licensing USA has agreed to allow their films be shown by license holders.

The Rules of the License

The most complicated rules of a public performance license have to do with how you are allowed to promote your film. Within the four walls of your library, you are allowed to promote a film as much and however you wish. However, when it comes to public advertising there are limits to what you can do and remain in compliance with the license. For public advertising of a film in newspapers, television, or radio—in other words, advertising that will likely reach people who are not cardholders in your system— you cannot use the title of the film or the studio or names of the director or actors in your advertising. The copyright companies highly recommend against public advertising such as the methods mentioned above.

Of all the guidelines stipulated by the licensing agreements, this is the one I get the most questions and hear the most frustration about, but do not panic! There are ways to create successful marketing and promotion for film programs while staying within these guidelines, and I will explore them in detail in chapter 7.

For some of us, the idea of big Hollywood studios seems a bit abstract. Why should they care if you run a film schedule in the local newspaper? Unless you work for a library in Southern California (and if you do, hello!), the chances of a studio exec happening in on your Saturday family movie program seems remote. But from the studio's perspective, a major part of protecting the intellectual property, or value, of a film is protecting its marketability. The local entity that would most likely be impacted by a public library film program is the local movie theater, the owner of which may well be aware of your Saturday family movie program.

Studios don't want libraries competing directly with theaters, and promising theaters that they will be protected from market competition by license holders is part of how they do that. If a library runs into trouble for violating the license agreement, it will almost certainly be because a local theater reported them to the studios. They are the ones who will see your publicity, and they are the ones who will, or will not, feel that you are crossing the line into direct competition with them.

The other thing to understand is that if for some reason—although I fervently hope you will avoid this—your library does run afoul of the marketing guidelines and find yourself reported to the studios or licensing company, you will not have violated federal law. You will have violated an agreement of understanding between yourself and the studios. Depending on the circumstances and how irritated the studios are, they may request you cancel your showing, pull your advertising, or, in extreme cases, demand your license be revoked. John Hill, from Movie Licensing USA, says, "Although this has not happened in Movie Licensing USA's ten years in existence, the major motion picture companies that we represent reserve the right to contact us at any time if they feel the need to pull a showing or pull the library's advertising for a showing" (John Hill, pers. comm.).

I offer this not to suggest the licenses shouldn't be taken seriously, but to put the reasons to follow them carefully into context. It is about maintaining a positive relationship with our "content suppliers" (the studios) and local businesses in our community.

A Little More about the Motion Picture Licensing Corporation ("MPLC") and Movie Licensing USA

Movie Licensing USA and the MPLC (Motion Picture Licensing Company) are the two main suppliers of public performance licenses to organizations. Each license covers a particular list of studios. There is some overlap of the studios covered in the two companies' licenses, but there are also some differences. Depending on the kind of programming you wish to offer, one company may serve your needs better, or you may wish to be covered by both.

Movie Licensing USA

10795 Watson Rd,
St. Louis, Missouri, 63127-1012
888-267-2658
Fax: 877-876-9873
www.movlic.com

Movie Licensing USA is owned by Swank Motion Pictures Inc., which specializes in nontheatrical distribution of motion pictures and public performance licensing. They serve a wide range, from libraries, schools, and churches to prisons, hospitals, and cruise lines and a number of other organizations in between. Movie Licensing USA is the branch of Swank Motion Pictures Inc. specifically focused on serving K–12 education and public libraries.

The studios covered by Movie Licensing USA, as of March 2013, are Columbia Pictures, DreamWorks Pictures, Fine Line Features, Focus Features, Hollywood Pictures, Lionsgate Films, MGM, Miramax Films, NBC/Universal Pictures, New Line Cinema, Sony Pictures, Summit Entertainment, Touchstone Pictures, TriStar Pictures, United Artists, Walt Disney Pictures, Warner Bros., and Warner Independent Pictures.

Movie Licensing USA also provides the option of one-time licenses for numerous studios not covered under their site license. These studios include, but are not limited to, A24 Films, CBS Films, Cohen Media Group, Entertainment One, Gaiam Vivendi Entertainment, Hallmark Hall of Fame, HBO, Image Entertainment, Magnolia Pictures, Millennium Entertainment, Monterey Media, Oscilloscope, Open Road Films, Relativity Media, and the Weinstein Company,

This one-time license is generally in the neighborhood of $100. If you are planning to show more than one movie in a year, the one-time license is not really worth it. But if you only occasionally show films, the one-time license may be an option. It can also be a way to expand your options if you have an umbrella license with MPLC. The one-time license from Movie Licensing USA could allow you access to one of the MLUSA films for a single program without buying the site license.

(Note: Although Movie Licensing USA requires that you get a one-time license to show these studios, a few of them, including Image Entertainment and Millennium Entertainment, are covered under the standard MPLC umbrella license.)

Movie Licensing USA has also recently begun to offer an anime license, which gives you access to screen the FUNimation catalog. The anime license is separate from the regular annual license, so even if you already have a Movie Licensing USA license, you must buy the anime license separately.

Movie Licensing USA offers a website that allows you to search titles to ensure they are covered by your license. They also provide downloadable posters and artwork that you can use in promoting your film programs. They provide phone support for questions and, according to John Hill, are happy to answer any questions, whether it's help determining if a film is covered, concerns about publicity, or suggestions for fund-raising.

Motion Picture Licensing Company

5455 Centinela Avenue
Los Angeles, CA 90066
800-462-8855
www.mplc.org

Motion Picture Licensing Company provides licenses to a wide array of organizations and businesses. Early in MPLC's history, they were very focused on the school and church market, which means that the list of studios covered by their license includes many smaller educational- and religion-focused studios, although that is not all they represent. Because they have cast a wide net to gather many smaller film companies, their license covers a wide range of television, educational, family, animation, independent, and foreign film producers, in addition to a few of the larger studios.

One important studio covered by MPLC to note—because it is the major large studio not covered by Movie Licensing USA—is Fox. All of the Fox subsidiaries, including Fox 2000, Fox-Look, Fox-Searchlight, and Fox-Walden, are covered by the MPLC license. MPLC's list of covered studios, available on their website, includes over one hundred studios, which I will not reproduce here. I will list several of the studios covered by the MPLC license that I believe would be particularly useful in a public library setting. They include (but are not limited to): A&E Channel, Animal Planet Video, Bard Entertainment, Bio Channel, British Film Institute, Cake Entertainment, Candlelight Media, Cartoon One, Castle Hill Productions, Discovery Channel Films, E! Entertainment Television, Echo Bridge Entertainment, Fangoria, FranceTV, Gateway/Vision Video, History Channel, ITV Global Entertainment, Image Entertainment, Jim Henson Productions, Learning Corporation of America, Lifetime Channel, London Film Productions, Merchant Ivory Productions, Military History Channel, Millennium Films, New Zealand Film Commission, Oregon Public Broadcasting, Oxford Film and Television, Scholastic Entertainment, Scottish Media Group, Sony Pictures Classic, and TLC Video.

The permissions granted by the MPLC license give you access to show an extensive selection of American and British television series and films, as well as anime, children's, and family films. It gives you access to the major motion pictures of the 20th Century Fox family of studios and of Sony Classic, the independent and international film branch of Sony Pictures.

The MPLC license is also less expensive than the Movie Licensing USA license, with costs ranging from $110 to $275 a year, depending on the population size of your service area. According to Sal Laudicina of the MPLC, the focus of the MPLC license is to provide a diverse list of studios and producers, ranging from Hollywood and independent studios to foreign producers. The MPLC recently added content from EGEDA, the nonprofit association and collection society that represents hundreds of producers from Spain and Latin America, representing over fifty thousand Spanish-language films and programs.

Unlike MLUSA, the MPLC never has films requiring a special license. "Any film from any of our studios is always covered," according to Sal Laudicina. MPLC also does not offer a "one-time showing" license. Laudicina says, "Our focus has always been offering the umbrella license, not licenses for individual screenings." He says that MPLC can work with systems to set up a shorter-term blanket license, if necessary (Sal Laudicina, pers. comm.). Contact the MPLC directly if you'd like to discuss options.

After many years of having a limited amount of help on their website, MPLC has recently and dramatically expanded the amount of information and customer support on their website. They provide studio lists and programming suggestions as well as customer support through the website or by phone.

I'd like to emphasize, regardless of license you may choose, the benefits of using the licensing company as a partner in your film programming. Take advantage of their customer service and websites. Call them with questions about titles or promotion. When I asked them both, John Hill from MLUSA and Sal Laudicina from MPLC were enthusiastically affirmative about libraries contacting them with any question relating to film programming.

Choosing Your License

In my opinion, the best possible option for choosing an umbrella license is to buy both a Movie Licensing USA and an MPLC license. This gives you the widest coverage, allowing you access to films from all the major studios, as well as permission to show films from smaller studios and television.

If you need to choose only one, you should review the kind of programming you think you would like to offer. The MLUSA license gives you access to almost all of the "big dog" studios, but not a lot of depth in smaller studio and television programming. The MPLC license limits your access to the major studios except for Fox, but allows you a wide array of smaller studios and television programming to choose from. If your focus is going to be primarily film programming for children, the MPLC license may be more than sufficient to cover your needs. If you wish to do a lot of feature film programming for all ages, the MLUSA license may work better for you.

Partnerships and Fund-Raising

Paying for licenses can be an opportunity to look at partnerships. When the Pierce County Library first began buying site licenses, it was in cooperation with Friends groups at a few branches. The Friends groups paid for the licenses and were also active in organizing and running the film programs. As the success of the film programs grew, the library system received support from the library foundation to expand and buy licenses for the whole system. Eventually the library was able to absorb the cost of purchasing licenses for all the branches into the regular budget, but in the early years of the system's film programming, support from the Friends and foundation were invaluable.

Both public performance rights and public performance licenses are designed to cover free screenings and explicitly state you cannot charge admission. There are still some options for fund-raising that you can take advantage of and still remain within the rules of the license.

If you have an umbrella license, you can sell tickets to film screenings up to the cost of the license. So if, for example, your library pays $500 for a license, you can sell tickets to recoup up to $500. You are also in the clear if you wish to collect donations during a screening or indicate a suggested donation at the door.

Collecting donations during a film screening can also provide an opportunity for library and community partnerships. The library can partner with local organizations that want to sponsor a movie night at the library. The group can raise funds via donations during the screening.

Movie Licensing USA offers a section on their website on how to raise funds through movie screenings under an umbrella license.[3] If you are showing a film with public performance rights rather than an umbrella license, I recommend contacting the film's supplier directly to ask about fund-raising options.

Occasionally an independent film is released and promoted as a fund-raising opportunity. In these cases, you are generally working directly with the filmmaker or studio that released the film. This can work out well for both parties, offering unique programming for your library and an opportunity to reach a wide audience for the filmmaker. I recommend, however, reviewing the details of the screening contract closely before committing. Sometimes the contracts require a set minimum ticket price or amount of money that you will be expected to pay the filmmaker or studio out of the profits. Understand the contract carefully before you commit, or you may end up raising more funds for the studio than for yourself.

A Word about Ratings

Ratings are not a legal issue, but they are often interpreted as one. Libraries deal with the issue of movie ratings not just in programming but every day. It is a complicated issue, especially for our patrons. Many of our patrons have erroneous assumptions about what ratings mean and what a library's role is in enforcing ratings. In discussing ratings I hope to give you a good understanding of them, since they are part of the inevitable landscape of film programming. I also wish to explore both their benefits and limitations.

The MPAA ratings system and the more recent TV Parental Guidelines have been designed by the Motion Picture Association of America and the television industry to help parents make decisions about what they wish their children to see.

Both the Motion Picture Association of America and the television industry groups that have developed TV ratings are private organizations. The rating system they have designed is a voluntary system with no force of state or federal law. Film and television studios submit their products to be rated voluntarily. When movie theaters or movie rental stores enforce ratings, they also do so voluntarily as private businesses.

The MPAA has historically fought long and hard to preserve the private, voluntary nature of this system. The MPAA has sued municipalities or states that have attempted to enforce ratings by law. The rating system is a form of self-regulation by the industry that has been designed to help parents and also safeguard artistic expression from government interference.[4]

The Ratings and What They Mean
MPAA Ratings[5]

G—The motion picture contains nothing that would offend parents for viewing by their children. There is minimal violence and no nudity, sex scenes, or drug use.

PG—Parents are urged to use "parental guidance," as the picture may contain some material parents might not like for their younger children to see. There may be some profanity and some depictions of violence, sensuality, or brief nudity, but "these elements are not deemed so intense as to require that parents be strongly cautioned beyond the suggestion of parental guidance." Additionally, there is no drug-use content.

PG-13—Parents are urged to be cautious. The picture may be inappropriate for preteenagers. There may be some profanity and some depictions of violence, sensuality, or brief nudity, but these elements are not deemed so intense as to require that parents be strongly cautioned beyond the suggestion of parental guidance. There is no drug-use content in a PG film.

R—Contains some adult material. "Parents are counseled to take this rating very seriously." Parents are urged to learn more about the film before taking their younger children with them. An R-rated film may depict adult activity, hard language, intense graphic or persistent violence, sexually oriented nudity, drug abuse, or other adult elements. "Generally, it is not appropriate for parents to bring their young children with them to R-rated movies."

NC-17—Patently adult. "NC-17 does not mean 'obscene' or 'pornographic' and should not be construed as a negative judgment" on the content of the film. "The rating simply signals that the content is appropriate only for an adult audience. An NC-17 rating can be based on violence, sex, aberrational behavior, drug abuse, or any other element that most parents would consider too strong for viewing by their children."

Television Industry Ratings

TV ratings include two parts: the audience designation, indicating the audience for which the program is most appropriate, and the content labels, which indicate the specific content a show may contain that might cause parental concern.

The content labels are:

> **D**—suggestive dialogue, often sexual in nature
> **L**—coarse or crude language
> **S**—sexual situations
> **V**—violence
> **FV**—fantasy violence (children's programming only)[6]

Content labels are paired with the following audience designations:

TVY—All Children. This program is designed to be appropriate for all children. Whether animated or live action, the themes and elements in this program are specifically designed for a very young audience, including children from ages 2 to 6. This program is not expected to frighten younger children.

TVY7—Directed to Older Children. This program is designed for children age 7 and above. It may be more appropriate for children who have acquired the developmental skills needed to distinguish between make-believe and reality. Themes and elements in this program may include mild fantasy violence or comedic violence, or may frighten children under the age of 7. Therefore, parents may wish to consider the suitability of this program for their very young children.

TVY7-FV—Directed to Older Children—Fantasy Violence. For those programs where fantasy violence may be more intense or more combative than other programs in this category, such programs will be designated TV-Y7-FV.

TVG—General Audience. Most parents would find this program suitable for all ages. Although this rating does not signify a program designed specifically for children, most parents may let younger children watch this program unattended. It contains little or no violence, no strong language and little or no sexual dialogue or situations.

PG—Parental Guidance Suggested. This program contains material that parents may find unsuitable for younger children. Many parents may want to watch it with their younger children. The theme itself may call for parental guidance and/or the program may contain one or more of the following: some suggestive dialogue (D), infrequent coarse language (L), some sexual situations (S), or moderate violence (V).

TV14—Parents Strongly Cautioned. This program contains some material that many parents would find unsuitable for children under 14 years of age. Parents are strongly urged to exercise greater care in monitoring this program and are cautioned against letting children under the age of 14 watch unattended. This program may contain one or more of the following: intensely suggestive dialogue (D), strong coarse language (L), intense sexual situations (S), or intense violence (V).

TVMA—Mature Audience Only. This program is specifically designed to be viewed by adults and therefore may be unsuitable for children under 17. This program may contain one or more of the following: crude indecent language (L), explicit sexual activity (S), or graphic violence (V).[7]

Motion picture and television ratings have been created to help parents in guiding their children's viewing experience. What ratings don't do is indicate in any way the quality of a program. They also don't necessarily identify every possible thing a viewer may object to. If someone is afraid of singing animals, a G rating is not going to do anything to help them.

Society has also changed over time, meaning that things that were considered shocking R-rated business in 1972 could easily earn a PG-13 or even PG rating today. It works the other way around as well. Things we consider important to protect children from today were once not given a second thought. Smoking used to be everywhere, including G-rated films, whereas today smoking guarantees a PG-13 rating. I recently watched the 1976 version of *The Bad News Bears*, which I had seen as a kid. I found my eyebrows flying off my head! Kids drinking, swearing, and smoking. Walter Matthau drinking and driving, and, for some reason most shocking to me, kids riding around in a car without wearing their seat belts!

It didn't change the fact that I thought it was a delightful film, but it did make me ponder how our expectations of behavior change over time. The film was rated PG in 1976. When it was remade in 2005, it received a PG-13 rating despite the fact that, for example, the character of Coach Buttermaker was not allowed by the MPAA ratings board to be seen drinking beer in the dugout,[8] something the character did plenty of in 1976.

It's important to keep in mind that in the history of film, ratings are a fairly recent development. The year 1968 is when the first MPAA ratings appeared, meaning there is almost sixty years' worth of films out there with no ratings at all. There are even more years without ratings for television, which didn't begin using ratings until the late 90s.

For films produced since 1969, it's also important to know that ratings are not mandatory. As mentioned before, the system was created to be a voluntary system, and no filmmaker is required to submit his or her film to the MPAA for review. Almost all films created by the big studios have ratings, but many smaller independent films, most foreign films, and many "direct to DVD" released films do not have ratings. The NR, or "Not Rated," designation means just that: it has not been submitted to the MPAA for review. It means nothing about the film's content; it is not the equivalent of an NC-17 or a G.

TIP
Regard Ratings as a Guide, Not a Rule

Ratings are a tool, but I urge any librarian designing a film program to use them as a guide rather than a definer of what to show. I believe there are films of almost any rating, including R or NR, that could be appropriate for a film program, providing you have a supportive audience for them. I also think that it's important that you review any film yourself before you show it to an audience, even if it's a Dove-certified G-rated family film. I don't think reviewing it would or should change your mind about showing it, but it allows you the confidence of knowing you will be prepared for anything that arises, even scenes of children riding around in open cars without their seat belts!

Rated R: Should You? Shouldn't You?

There are many great films that are rated R, and an R rating should not automatically disqualify you from selecting a film for viewing. That said, it is also very important that you honestly assess your own community before deciding what films to show, regardless of rating. Certain communities will not blink if the library film program features an R film, but others will. If you live and work in those communities, you should know the difference. If you work for a multibranch system, you may have both kinds of communities, each with different tolerances. It's important to respect those tolerances.

John Fossett, the collection services manager for Kitsap Regional Library in Bremerton, Washington, has run film programs for KRL for many years. Here's what he has to say about showing R films:

> In regard to considering film ratings for film programs it depends on the community. At [Branch A] we have shown a couple of R-rated films, but only after we had the program going for a while and had established an audience. It hasn't been an issue.

However, at [Branch B] they tend to stick with more family-friendly productions. I don't think an R-rated movie would do well there. That's why it's important to include the branch manager in the film selection process. They not only know their community, but they'll be the first to hear a complaint if one is lodged (John Fossett, pers. comm.).

Remember that screening films is ultimately about creating an enjoyable, entertaining program for your patrons. When promoting a film program, include the rating. Specify the library's intended audience for the film. Is it for children? All ages? Teens? Adults? The more information you include—including the ratings—the less likely you will have a patron upset or angered by a film program experience. Give patrons the information they need so they can select a program that's right for them.

Notes

1. "Public Performance Law," Motion Picture Association of America, accessed January 18, 2013, www.mpaa.org/contentprotection/public-performance-law.
2. "Order Information: Rental," Bullfrog Films, accessed January 18, 2013 www.bullfrogfilms.com/orderinfo.html#rental.
3. "Fundraising Ideas for Your Film Program," Movie Licensing USA Public Libraries, accessed February 14, 2014, http://library.movlic.com/fundraisingIdeas.
4. "Ratings History," Motion Picture Association of America, accessed January 18, 2013, www.mpaa.org/ratings/ratings-history.
5. The wording for this section is taken from the following sources: "Film Ratings," Classification & Rating Administration (CARA), accessed January 18, 2013, www.filmratings.com/filmRatings_Cara/#/ratings; "About Us," Classification & Rating Administration (CARA), accessed January 18, 2013, www.filmratings.com/filmRatings_Cara/#/about; "What Each Rating Means," Motion Picture Association of America, accessed January 18, 2013, www.mpaa.org/ratings/what-each-rating-means.
6. The TV Parental Guidelines (website), accessed January 18, 2013, www.tvguidelines.org/index.htm.
7. Ibid.
8. *IMDB*, sv "Bad News Bears (2005)," accessed January 18, 2013, www.imdb.com/title/tt0408524/trivia.

MARKETING

With marketing, as with everything else in public libraries, we wrestle with constraints of time and budget. We struggle to figure out the best ways to focus our marketing so that it reaches the audience that will most benefit from our programs. We have all experienced throwing everything but the kitchen sink toward promoting a program only to have three people show up, and many of us have also experienced a halfhearted flyer bringing throngs to a program we only thought would have three. We are thrilled when a heavily marketed program brings a good turnout and then baffled when the following month, with the same marketing, no one shows up.

Successful marketing any program for your library, be it film or otherwise, is the holy grail. Traditional marketing techniques for libraries often include posters, flyers, calendars, mailings (both e- and snail), and, if budget allows, newspaper or radio ads. Meanwhile, the Internet and social media are providing new ways of reaching out to our patrons, and new social media applications are being invented every day.

In most respects, marketing a film program is like marketing any other program. But there is a significant difference. When marketing film programs, libraries must stay compliant with their film license, and it is in respect to marketing that film licenses seem to have the most limitations.

It's reasonable to feel that these limitations severely tie one's hands in the kind of promotion that is available for film programs. But there are ways to successfully promote a film program while remaining in compliance, including many social media options.

Although we discussed these limitations in chapter 5, let's look at them again. Here is the information from the "Advertising" page of the Movie Licensing USA website (http://library.movlic.com/guidelines):

Advertising to Patrons/Cardholders Inside Your Library

Within your facility, you are free to advertise the movie title, studio, actors and artwork (as long as it includes the studio's copyright, for example: ©Walt Disney Pictures).

You may also send correspondence directly to your card holders that includes all movie information, for example, patron mailings, e-mails and monthly newsletters.

Advertising to Non-Cardholders/General Public

If you choose to advertise through public media (such as public radio, television, newspaper or a website), you may do so, as long as your message does not include the movie title and studio name. For example, "Join us at Anytown Library for a Neighborhood Movie Night at 7:00pm" is permitted.

So, that's irritating. If you want to put an ad in a local paper, on the radio, or if you want to hang up posters outside the library, you can't use the film title, director, stars, or studio. Marketing programs within the library is an important part of any promotion, but how do we get the word out to the person who doesn't visit the library regularly but would be thrilled to hear about your upcoming movie program?

Before we go further, let's examine why these restrictions are in place. Not to be tedious, but in understanding the reasons for these restrictions, we can get some very helpful clues to navigate these limitations, remain fully in compliance, and still create exciting film promotions.

The first reason these limitations are in place is that the studios want to limit the library's ability to compete directly with local movie theaters. It's true that movie theaters are showing first-run feature films while we are obviously limited to titles no longer in theaters. But the fact remains that your local theater does not want to see an ad in the local paper that says, "Come See *Captain America* Free at the Smithtown Public Library" next to their ad for *The Avengers*. A patron might look at your ad, and then at the movie theater ad, and find themselves thinking, *Well, you know, I didn't really want to spend fifty dollars to take the family out tonight. And you know, if the library is showing* Captain America *now, maybe they're going to show* The Avengers *later, and the snacks at the theater are so expensive, and the last time I went there the parking was terrible . . .* "Hey, kids! Get in the car! We're going to the library!"

Now that is clearly a win for us! But your local theater sees that as direct competition. Not only are they not going to show a movie for free, the fact is they generally can't show a movie for free. Movie theaters have complicated agreements with studios regarding revenues and how much money they have to send back to the studios before the local theater can even start to earn a profit. Movie theaters are in competition with each other. They're in competition with cable, On Demand, RedBox, Netflix, and the grocery store down the street. They *can't* do much about that, but they can certainly make an irate phone call to a studio about the taxpayer-funded library down the street that's trying to muscle in on their business.

The other aspect of why your license limits advertising to the general public has to do with what you have paid for. The cost of your license is based on the population of your service area. In other words, you have paid to be allowed to show films to the people in your service area. Broad-spectrum advertising—such as in newspapers, on the radio, or on a poster in the grocery store—will likely reach people who are not in your service area.

As a comparison, it might be helpful to think about electronic databases. Generally the cost of a database is based on your service population or circulation. The database usually requires that patrons are authenticated—by entering their library card number, for example—before they can access the database. This is how a database company makes sure that the library is using what it has paid for, which is access to that database for its patrons, and not access to that database for anyone who wants to use it regardless of where they are from.

In this respect, film licensors are savvy enough to know that, unlike with databases, the library is not generally demanding attendees show a library card to attend a public program. So, from the licensor's perspective, preventing the library from advertising a specific film by name in advertising to the general public is their way of limiting (but not demanding we eliminate entirely) the number of people from outside our service area who come to see a film.

There is one legal way around the "no title" prohibition in advertising to the general public, and that is what I call the "based-on" exception. If you are showing a film that is based on a book, you can use the title of the *book* in your advertising. It is just fine to advertise: "Come see the award-winning film based on the best-selling book *The Help* this Friday at 7 pm."

Even with the "based-on" exception, it is difficult to effectively advertise to the general public with the title/actor/studio limitation of the film license. This limitation takes newspaper ads, radio ads, and public posters out of play except for general promotions for "movie nights" or "film series."

So the question becomes: If we're limited to advertising to the general public, how do we focus our promotions to our patrons? Are in-house posters and flyers all that are available to us? The answer is decidedly no, and that is thanks in part to the wonderful world of the Internet and social media. The main goal with any medium is to focus on how to promote programs directly to our registered patrons.

Direct Notification

It's not particularly glamorous, but mailing flyers of film programs to patrons is totally acceptable. E-mailing patrons is also acceptable.

The Library Website

The library's website is an interesting animal. It is decidedly public. Anyone can visit it, after all. But the licensors acknowledge that there is a difference between the home page of a website and the levels behind it. It's not OK to place a promotion for a film program using the title on your home page. It is all right, however, to list detailed program information further in. So you could, for example, have a banner on your website that says "Film Program Thursday Night" that links to a detailed description, including the title, actors, studio, and so forth.

Detailed film program information can be shared on program pages or calendars. If your youth services department has its own subpage and is running film programs, those programs can be promoted there. If you are part of a system with branches, each of which has their own subpage, you can promote film programs on the branch page.

A very good example of using a website to successfully promote film programs is the New York City Public Library page (www.nypl.org). On the NYPL home page there is a drop-down link for programs under "Classes & Events." This takes you to a complete list of all their programs, including film. It being NYPL, there are a lot of programs (over six thousand when I was visiting today!), but you can narrow down by film programs under "All Programs." Here's what it looks like:

WEDNESDAY, MAY 23, 2012

2 p.m.	Showtime! Children's Films	Stephen A. Schwarzman Building, Children's Center at 42nd Street	Children, Toddlers (18–36 months), Pre-schoolers (3–5 years), School Age (5–12 years)
4 p.m.	Tyler Perry Film Series: Madea Goes to Jail First come, first served	Countee Cullen Library, Auditorium	Adults, 50+, College & Graduate Students

THURSDAY, MAY 24, 2012

2 p.m.	Cinema Thursdays @ the Riverdale Library	Riverdale Library	Adults, 50+
2 p.m.	Film: FEATURING DORIS DAY	96th Street Library	Adults
3 p.m.	Teen Movie Night	Tompkins Square Library,	Teens/Young Adults (13–18 years)
4 p.m.	Movies @ Kips Bay Library presents New Releases Movie Night: War Horse	Kips Bay Library	Adults

Source: New York Public Library, www.nypl.org/events/calendar.

A click on any of these brings you to more information:

Movies @ Kips Bay Library Presents
New Releases Movie Night: War Horse

Thursday, May 24, 2012, 4–6 p.m.
PROGRAM LOCATIONS:
Kips Bay Library (Map and directions)
Fully accessible to wheelchairs
Jeremy Irvine, Emily Watson, David Thewlis; Directed by Steven Spielberg;
146 mins; 2011

Set against a sweeping canvas of rural England and Europe during the First World War, "War Horse" begins with the remarkable friendship between a horse named Joey and a young man called Albert, who tames and trains him. When they are forcefully parted, the film follows the extraordinary journey of the horse as he moves through the war, changing and inspiring the lives of all those he meets.

Source: New York Public Library, www.nypl.org/events/calendar.

The page also provides links that allow a patron to tweet, post on Facebook, or e-mail information about the program.

Social Media

The idea of using social media tools may seem antithetical to this whole notion of not promoting specific information to the general public. If social media such as Twitter or Facebook is anything, it's public, right? Well, yes but no. If the library has a Twitter account, it can tweet information about programs to its followers. Despite appearances, that tweet does not actually go out to the whole world. It goes out to the library's followers: people who have signed up to receive tweets specifically from the library. The fact that followers have actively signed up to receive information from the library is enough, from our licensors' perspective, to reassure them that those are your patrons.

The library can also use a Facebook page to promote film programs, for the same reason. For someone on Facebook to receive postings from the library, they have to visit your page and "friend" you. This action of friending the library reassures the licensors that the person seeing your promotion is not a random nonresident passerby who, for example, just happened to see a poster in the grocery store and thought they'd stop in at your film program.

TIP
Reach Out to Your Local Theater

One step libraries can take to help make promoting film programs easier is to contact the local movie theater. Since it is the theater that would be most likely to take exception to something your library is doing—even if it's something well within the bounds of the license—reaching out to your local theaters to tell them about your program plans or alert them to any special film related events can be beneficial. The more your local theater is familiar with the library, the more they will understand the public service mission of your programs and the less likely they are to be surprised or react negatively to a film program.

Marketing

Now that you have some ideas of what tools to use to promote your film program, let's talk about what to include in publicity for your film programs. Some of this may seem obvious, but it can be easy to overlook in the rush of putting out flyers or getting something posted to your calendar.

Definitely include:

- location
- time
- length of film
- intended audience

Consider including:

- rating
- food/no food allowed
- suggested donation amount (if accepted)
- discussion before or after

Identifying Your Audience

Film programs are great for all ages, but not *all* film programs are great for all ages. Identifying the intended audience for film programming is helpful to both you and your patrons. Is your upcoming Bugs Bunny marathon intended as a children's program? Bugs has fans of all ages, so you might end up with a very mixed audience. This isn't necessarily a big deal, but forewarned is forearmed. You don't want to have a difficult conversation with an older patron who reverently came to see the Warner Brothers cartoon canon and is now upset that there are all these noisy kids running around. The more your patrons know about the program in advance, the better.

Clearly identifying the audience in your marketing materials is particularly important for programs in which age plays a role in who can attend. Obviously if you are showing an R-rated film or film with intense content, you want to make it clear that the program is intended for adults. This works the other way too. If a child must have a parent or caregiver with them to attend a program, you need to make that clear in the marketing. If an adult must have a child with them to attend a program, you need to make that clear in the marketing. If grown-ups "aren't allowed" in your teen movie treehouse, you need to make that clear in the marketing.

Several of my friends who are teen librarians have told me about a growing challenge with what they call "reluctant graduates" of teen programs. Many young adults in their late teens and early 20s still love the same things they did when they were teens, such as anime or gaming, but few parents are going to be comfortable with a teen film night that has attendees in their early 20s. If your system has a large enough population of late-teen/early-20s residents, you might consider starting film programming especially for them. But in the meantime, it's important to establish age guidelines for attendees of programs. Providing these details in your marketing materials won't necessarily stop difficult situations from arising, but if they do arise, you will be able to easily refer to the flyer to explain to your enthusiastic "reluctant graduate" why they can't come to teen film night anymore.

Evaluating Your Program

How to evaluate library programs, including film programs, is the $64,000 question. It is important that we thoughtfully assess our programs to ensure that they are meeting customer need. We also need to be able to show that they are a reasonable use of library resources, including staff time.

There are lots of different ways to evaluate programs. Some are very numbers and data driven. Others are about getting feedback, "taking the temperature of the room," and other tools that are very useful but can feel less concrete to those who want a chart and a graph that gives them a definitive yes-or-no answer to the question "Should we continue with this program?"

In *Basic Guide to Program Evaluation* (Including Outcomes Evaluation), Carter McNamara says, "Many people believe that evaluation is about proving the success or failure of a program. This myth assumes that success is implementing the perfect program and never having to hear from employees, customers or clients again—the program will now run itself perfectly. This doesn't happen in real life. Success is remaining open to continuing feedback and adjusting the program accordingly. Evaluation gives you this continuing feedback."[1]

Evaluating a program is a three-step process: establish your goals and targets, gather evaluations and data from the programs, and compare your goals and outcome. Using these steps, you can establish a method to evaluate your program that ensures that everyone is using the same goalposts to measure success.

- Establish goals and targets.
  - Identify the kind of audience(s) you wish to reach (kids, teens, adults, etc.).
  - Identify the size of audience you hope to reach with the program.

- ○ Identify the scope of the program. (one time only, weekly, monthly, etc.).
- ○ Identify the staff commitment the library is able to support.
- Evaluate program outcomes.
  - ○ Count attendees.
  - ○ Get evaluations and feedback from customers and staff.
  - ○ Measure staff time.
- Compare goals and outcomes.
  - ○ Decide if you are on target, if you need to adjust, or if you need to rethink.

Setting Goals and Targets

The first step in evaluating your program is deciding what your goals are for the program. Is a full house a sign of a great success? Or is it a sign that you booked too small a room? Are five attendees at your film discussion group a failure? Or is five the perfect size for everyone to participate? Can you pull off a successful regular film program along with your other duties? Or does it swallow your time and the library's resources, leaving you unable to complete other work or present other programs?

Establishing ahead of time what your goals are for the program is essential to being able to fairly evaluate it. It can help minimize crossed wires between yourself, your colleagues, and your supervisor. It can help you decide if a program is worth pursuing or if it needs to be reconsidered.

Once you've set a goal, you can use targets to measure whether a program is working. You can set a target of a minimum number of attendees, or a minimum amount of attendee increase per program (a minimum of three more attendees each program, for example). You can set targets to evaluate the time staff put into creating a program. The first time you put together a new program, for example, it may take a great deal of time. When I am working on developing the Pierce County Reads film lists, it can take me three or four hours a day for four or five days. But you can set a target that the staff time to set things up will be no more than two hours a week by six weeks into the program.

If a program isn't meeting a target, it doesn't mean that anyone is failing. It means that the format of the program needs to be adjusted or that goals must be reassessed. Targets help you evaluate whether the goals are attainable. Targets shouldn't be used as "sticks," but as ways for the library to measure success, and to make sure that everyone is using the same goals to measure success.

Evaluating Program Outcomes
Counting Noses

The most straightforward way of evaluating the success of your program is counting turnout. Turnout is important, and everyone dreams of a full house for all their programs. But this is one place where establishing your goals is important. Evaluating your program will be much easier for you and your supervisors if you are clear about how big an audience you feel is necessary to consider the program a success.

Aside from straight numbers, there are other ways you can evaluate your program based on attendance. If your program is a series, did people return? Did they bring friends and family? Are they asking for information about future programs? Is your audience growing? Are people staying through the whole program, participating, and asking questions at the end? All of these are signs that you are on to something with your program. Patrons are coming back, and they are helping you build your audience.

Evaluation Forms

A good place to start evaluating any program is for your library to create a program evaluation form, a survey that is given to attendees of every program. Creating a program evaluation form establishes a standardized tool that all your library programs can use to measure success.

This form is designed to be used for any program at PCLS, not just film programs. If you do enough film programs, you may want to consider a focused survey that asks film-specific questions. In the case of PCLS, however, staff find that they are able get the feedback they need from this general survey.

Tami Masenhimer, community supervisor for the Fife branch of the Pierce County Library, uses the event evaluation form to help her gauge program success and plan new programs. "I look at what people have to say in the free text portions. [I] usually find the 'I didn't like this' more informative that the 'I liked this.' It gives me guidance in how I can improve or change things up" (Tami Masenhimer, pers. comm.).

This is an example of the program evaluation form used by the Pierce County Library:

Event Evaluation

Pierce County Library location _____

Event _____

Date _____

Thank you for your comments to help Pierce County Library System improve events and services for you.

On a scale of 1 to 5 (5 being the highest), please rate the following items:
1. Overall quality of the event. 1 2 3 4 5
2. The event was smart, fun, friendly. 1 2 3 4 5
3. The length of the event was: Too long _____ Too short _____ Just right _____
4. What's the most effective method to notify you of events like this?
   (Circle all that apply)
   E-mail   Newspaper advertisements   Twitter
   Facebook   News stories   Website
   Flyer/info in library   Online advertisements   Whiteboard in library
   Flyer/info outside library   Other _____
5. How did you learn of today's event? (Circle all that apply)
   E-mail   Newspaper advertisements   Twitter
   Facebook   News stories   Website
   Flyer/info in library   Online advertisements   Whiteboard in library
   Flyer/info outside library   Other _____
6. How many times have you visited a Pierce County Library in the past 12 months?
   1 2 3 4 5 6+
7. Do you have a library card? Yes No
   If you live in the service area and haven't gotten one, get one today!

Further comments _____
_____

To join the library's e-mail listserv for information about events and issues, please write your name and e-mail address: _____
_____

PCLS 40 MCR 3/13 (1200)

Using Feedback

Whether you use an evaluation form or ask your patrons directly, get feedback from them about the programs. Ask them! One of the real benefits in asking patrons about your film programs is that it can also be an opportunity to promote your next film program. Miguel Colon, assistant supervisor for the Sumner branch of the Pierce County Library, says, "For our Bilingual Family Movie Nights, I discuss the movie of choice with the parents and families as they visit our library. That way the kids get an opportunity to give their input and the parents have a chance to give their blessings. Then on the actual movie night . . . I will ask the group if they have any suggestions on what our next movie should be. I usually get good participation, and this way I know we're showing something that they are interested in viewing" (Miguel Colon, pers. comm.).

In addition to what she finds out from evaluation forms, Masenhimer also gathers direct feedback from film audiences to help design her programs. Masenhimer says, "I [ask] for themes, or sometimes ask if next time they would like to see a film about 'x' or 'y.' By giving [them] an either/or [question] I am not opening it up so wide that I can't provide a quality program, but am still letting the group give direction. For example, I may ask, 'For next time we will discuss minorities in film. Would you like to study the portrayals of Native American in early western films, or the portrayals of African Americans in musicals of the 1950s?'" (Tami Masenhimer, pers. comm.)

Customer Experience and Your Own

During the program, you can observe how things are going. These observations are an important part of evaluating the success of a program. Are program attendees engaged? Are they distracted, or distracting others? Are people staying for the whole program or wandering in and out?

Programs that have a discussion or question-and-answer period afterward also provide opportunity for evaluation. John Fossett says about film discussion groups: "I like to see people engaged and participating. Not everyone has to talk, but you want them following the discussion, not texting or updating their Facebook status. In addition to the number of people attending and participating, I look at the quality of the discussion. Did it stay on point (i.e., centered around themes and ideas represented in the movie)? Did it veer off into the ether and settle on something way beyond the scope of the work? (The moderator should steer those diversions back toward the track.) Is there exchange between attendees? I find the best discussions occur when some like the work and some don't. As long as it's respectful I let [the conversation] go" (John Fossett, pers. comm.).

The programs that we do are for the appreciation and edification of our customers. But I believe it's totally reasonable to ask ourselves how *we* liked the program. You can usually tell if you feel like a program is going well or poorly, and you can also tell if you are enjoying giving the program, or if it's causing you misery and despair. If you find that you are having a terrible time, that could be a good indicator that perhaps there's something about the program that's not clicking.

I once volunteered to take over a film discussion group for the regular moderator who was on vacation. I researched the film in advance, came prepared with notes, watched the film with the group, and then proceeded to "lead" the discussion. I asked the group what they thought of the film. Silence. I rambled a bit about what I thought of the film. Uncomfortable silence. In the end I acknowledged that it didn't seem like we had much to say about it, so perhaps we should cut it short. Everyone bolted from the room. It was terrible!

Fortunately for me, the regular leader was back the next month, so I didn't have to try it again with that group. But it was still a good lesson for me. I now realize that particular group was already a "group" which I was not regularly a part of. They had, in fact, already been chatting when I sat down with them and pulled out my Librarian Notes and began to try to "lead the class." If I had a chance to do it again, I'd do a lot more listening and a lot less leading for that particular group of people. A different group might have wanted more guidance from a leader, but in that instance I failed to read the room.

I've since learned that "leading" a discussion group is really about getting out of the conversation's way. You should guide the conversation if it seems to be going off track, or offer prompts if it's dragging, but the group should be talking more than you. Having that terrible experience helped me realize there was something I was missing that I needed to learn.

If you have a lousy experience with a program, it's often because you have a different notion of what the program is than the attendees do. That may be on them, or it may be on you, but since they're the customer, you're the one that needs to rethink the program. Do you need to be showing different films? Do you need to explain better in the promotional materials what the program is meant to be? Are you reaching the right audience? Do you need to be providing a program for the audience you have, rather than the one you wish you had?

Although we all want all our programs to be successful, occasionally we will all have a miss. When the misses happen, use them as a chance to learn. Today's uncomfortable silence can be tomorrow's well-loved program.

Measuring Staff Time

We work in a profession that loves data and metrics. Numbers on a page are a great way to show busy finance directors, library directors, and board members that programs are valuable. But how do you get an equation out of a program?

John Fossett from Kitsap Regional Library uses a formula for measuring the cost of film programs that is a very useful tool these days when hard numbers and metrics are so important. Track your hours of staff time prepping for and presenting the program. Multiply the hours by your pay rate and divide it by the number of attendees to establish the cost per patron.

$$\text{program cost formula} = \\ \text{(staff hours prepping and presenting program)} \times \text{(pay rate)} \\ \div \text{(\# of attendees)}$$

Kitsap uses this formula to evaluate all programs, including summer reading, and they like to keep program costs to $2 per person or less for staff time and materials. Of course, there are variables that will impact turnout, such as branch size, intended audience, focus of the program, competing events in the community, and even the weather. Many a wonderful program at a Pacific Northwest library has been undone by an unexpectedly beautiful day!

"It can be a challenge," Fossett says, "to stay within [the $2] parameter when programming at some of our smaller branches. However, the cost averages out respectably when we have a huge turnout at one of the bigger branches" (John Fossett, pers. comm.).

Evaluating a program can seem daunting and rather nebulous, but by establishing your goals and targets, gathering evaluations and data, and comparing your goals and outcomes, you can establish a consistent means of evaluating programs. Use these steps to establish an evaluation method that ensures that everyone is using the same goalposts to measure success.

Note

1. Carter McNamara, "Basic Guide to Program Evaluation (Including Outcomes Evaluation)," Free Management Library, accessed April 8, 2013, http://managementhelp.org/evaluation/program-evaluation-guide.htm.

APPENDIX A
Films Based on Books for Children

The Adventures of Huck Finn (1993; Disney, PG)

Elijah Wood and Courtney B. Vance star in this heavy on adventure, light (though not completely absent) on message version of the Mark Twain classic.

American Girl series

The American Girl doll begat a series of books about plucky industrious girls in American history, and these books have now begat their own film adaptations. *Samantha: An American Girl Holiday, Felicity: An American Girl Adventure, Molly: An American Girl On the Homefront,* and *Chrissa: An American Girl Stands Strong* are all made-for-TV movies shown on the Disney Channel and HBO. *Kit Kittredge: An American Girl* (2008; New Line Cinema, G) is a major motion picture starring Abigail Breslin.

Ballet Shoes (2007; BBC, PG)

Noel Stretfield's classic tale of the trials and tribulations of Pauline, Petrova, and Posy Fossil in a BBC adaptation starring Emma Watson.

Because of Winn-Dixie (2005; 20th Century Fox, PG)

Adaptation of the Kate DiCamillo novel, starring Jeff Daniels, Cicely Tyson, Dave Matthews, and a very cute dog.

The Black Cauldron (1985; Disney, G)

The only book of Lloyd Alexander's Prydain series to be adapted into film, this animated feature tells the adventure of assistant pig-keeper Taran and his oracular pig Hen Wen.

Bridge to Terabithia (2007; Disney, PG)

Novelist Katherine Paterson was inspired by the vivid imaginary world of her son David to write the beloved children's novel. Thirty years later, David Paterson wrote the screenplay for this film.

Charlotte's Web (1973; Paramount, G)

For most titles on this list I tried to limit to a single adaptation, but I'm afraid in this case I'm a purist of the old school, and my heart belongs to the 1973 animated version of *Charlotte's Web*. However, I understand the 2006 live-action version, also from Paramount and also rated G, is quite delightful.

Chitty Chitty Bang Bang (1968; United Artists, G)

It wasn't all dry martinis for Ian Fleming, who wrote this delightful tale of a flying car for his young son. The screenplay for the film version was adapted by beloved author Roald Dahl.

City of Ember (2008; Playtone, PG)

Cinematic adaptation of the first book in Jeanne DuPrau's Book of Ember series, about two teenagers attempting to escape from a dying underground city.

Cloudy with a Chance of Meatballs (2009; Columbia, PG)

Animated adaptation of the beloved children's book by Judi Barrett.

Coraline (2009; Focus Features, PG)

Neil Gaiman's creepy book about a girl who longs for more perfect parents—until she gets them—is given the creepy stop-motion animation treatment.

Curious George (2006; Universal, G)

The intrepid monkey is given the animated treatment, with the voice of Will Ferrell as "the Man with the Yellow Hat."

Diary of a Wimpy Kid series

Based on Jeff Kinney's books about the adventures of Geff Heffley, who faithfully records the indignities of middle-school in his diary—I mean JOURNAL: *The Diary of a Wimpy Kid* (2010; 20th Century Fox, PG), *Diary of a Wimpy Kid: Roderick Rules* (2011; Fox 2000, PG), and *Diary of a Wimpy Kid: Dog Days* (2012; Fox 2000, PG).

Ella Enchanted (2004; Miramax, PG)

Film version of Gail Carson Levine's Newbery Honor book about a feisty girl cursed with the "gift" of obedience, complete with adorable song-and-dance numbers.

Escape to Witch Mountain (1975; Disney, G)

Film based on the exciting sci-fi novel by Alexander Key about two children with special powers trying to find their way home. Disney adapted the story again in 2005 as *Race to Witch Mountain*.

The Fantastic Mr. Fox **(2009; 20th Century Fox, PG)**

Stop-motion animated version of the Roald Dahl story.

The Great Mouse Detective **(1986; Disney, G)**

Based on the book *Basil of Baker Street* by Eve Titus and in the tradition of Sherlock Holmes, Basil the Great Mouse Detective must save the queen from his arch-nemesis, the evil Ratigan.

The Hideaways **(1973; Warner Home Video, G)**

Film adaptation of *From the Mixed-Up Files of Mrs. Basil E. Frankweiler* by E. L. Konisburg about runaways hiding in the Metropolitan Museum of Art.

Harriet the Spy **(1996; Paramount, PG)**

Film adaptation of Louise Fitzhugh's book about precocious Harriet and her spy notebook.

Holes **(2003; Disney, PG)**

Louis Sachar's story of the misnamed Camp Green Lake, the evil warden, the intrepid Stanley Yelnats IV, and holes, lots and lots of holes.

How to Eat Fried Worms **(2006; New Line Cinema, PG)**

A 9-year-old viewer of *How To Eat Fried Worms* was heard to say, "This is really disgusting, but I like it!" The movie is truthful to the spirit, if not exactly the story, of the original book.

Hugo **(2011; Paramount, PG)**

Brian Selznick's beautiful novel *The Invention of Hugo Cabret* convinced Martin Scorsese that it was finally time for him to direct a family picture, and five Academy Awards were the result. Incredibly faithful to the magic of the book.

The Indian in the Cupboard **(1995; Sony, PG)**

Frank Oz directed this adaptation of the novel by Lynne Reid Banks.

James and the Giant Peach **(1996; Disney, PG)**

The stop-motion animation and direction by Henry Selick, who also directed *The Nightmare before Christmas*, capture well the creepy magic of Roald Dahl's story.

Judy Moody and the Not Bummer Summer **(2011; Relativity Media, PG)**

Based on Megan McDonald's Judy Moody series.

Jumanji **(1995; Sony, PG)**

Robin Williams stars in this adaptation of Chris Van Allsburg's picture book about a board game that comes to life.

The Last Unicorn (1982; Lion's Gate, G)

Animated adaptation of the novel by Peter S. Beagle about a unicorn who goes on a quest to find out what has happened to all the other unicorns.

Matilda (1996; Sony, PG)

Another Roald Dahl tale adapted to the screen, directed by and starring Danny DeVito.

Millions (2004; 20th Century Fox, PG)

Based on the Carnegie Medal winner *Millions* by Frank Cottrell Boyce and directed by Danny Boyle, this film is about two brothers who find a bag of money and must decide what to do with it—before the robbers catch up with them.

Nancy Drew (2007; Warner Bros, PG)

After a spate of Nancy Drew film adaptations in the 1930s, the intrepid girl detective disappeared from the big screen for almost seventy years!

Nanny McPhee (2005; Universal, PG)

Christianna Brand's *Nurse Matilda* books became *Nanny McPhee* for the big screen.

Night at the Museum (2006; 20th Century Fox, PG)

Milan Trenc's picture book is brought to life as rip-roaring adventure.

The Phantom Tollbooth (1970; MGM, G)

Animated adaptation of the book by Norton Juster.

The Polar Express (2004; Warner Bros, PG)

Chris Van Allsburg's beautiful Christmas picture book adapted to film using motion-capture animation.

Pollyanna

Eleanor H. Porter's tale of the optimistic orphan has been adapted to film many times for both the big screen, television, and even Japanese anime. The 1960 Disney version starring Hayley Mills is considered the gold standard by many.

Ramona and Beezus (2010; 20th Century Fox, G)

Beverly Cleary's beloved Ramona series makes it to the big screen in this well-reviewed adaptation.

The Rescuers (1977; Disney, G)

Margery Sharpe's tale of the brave and beautiful Miss Bianca and the Rescue Aid Society, brought to life by Disney and voiced by Eva Gabor.

The Secret of NIMH (1982; MGM, G)

Based on *Mrs. Frisby and the Rats of NIMH* by Robert C. O'Brien, about a plucky mouse and some highly intelligent rats. The movie is pretty true to the book, except for the introduction of a "magic amulet," which to a lover of the book really seems quite unnecessary.

The Secret World of Arrietty (2010; Distributed by Disney, G)

Lovers of *The Borrowers* by Mary Norton will have no problem identifying the inspiration for this Japanese animated fantasy. In fact, in Japanese it was titled *The Borrower Arrietty*, but in a mystery known only to Hollywood, all reference to *The Borrowers* was dropped from the English title. *The Borrowers* was also adapted to film in 1997 starring John Goodman (Universal, PG).

Shrek (2001; Dreamworks, PG)

William Steig wrote and illustrated the picture book *Shrek*, about a terrifying ogre who decides to venture out and see the world. The rest is history.

Skellig (2009; Image Entertainment, PG)

Film adaptation of the Prinz Honor book *Skellig* by David Almond, about a boy who discovers a mysterious man with special powers living in the garage.

Stuart Little (1999; Sony, PG)

Rather loosely adapted but still entertaining film from the classic book by E. B. White.

The Sword in the Stone (1963; Disney, G)

Disney adaptation of T. H. White's *The Once and Future King*.

The Tale of Desperaux (2008; Universal, G)

Kate DiCamillo's fantasy adventure of a mouse who longs for adventure brought to the big screen.

Tom Sawyer (1973; United Artists, G)

A musical version of the Mark Twain classic starring Johnny Whitaker, a face familiar to anyone older than 30 for his role in *Sigmund and the Sea Monsters* and also a young Jodie Foster as Becky.

The Unidentified Flying Oddball (1979; Disney, G)

Mark Twain's *A Connecticut Yankee in King Arthur's Court* has had numerous film adaptations, but only one featuring a robot named Hermes.

A Wish for Wings That Work (1991; Universal, NR)

Made-for-television adaptation of Berkley Breathed's holiday tale of Opus the Penguin and his dreams of flight.

APPENDIX B
Year-Round Film Programming Ideas

There are many resources on the Internet for guides to the special days and holidays of every month. I like Holiday Insights (holidayinsights.com). As for the films on this list, they are titles I think could work for a particular theme, but none of these lists are exhaustive.

January

January features National Letter Writing Week, a surprisingly fruitful topic for film.

- *The Shop around the Corner* (1940; MGM, NR)
  Jimmy Stewart and Margaret Sullivan are coworkers who despise each other, little knowing they are falling in love through letters as anonymous pen pals. *The Shop around the Corner* inspired the Tom Hanks/Meg Ryan hit *You've Got Mail*.
- *84 Charing Cross Road* (1987; Columbia, PG)
  Anne Bancroft and Anthony Hopkins star in this delightful film about two lonely book lovers who establish a profound friendship via letters.
- *The Love Letter* (1999; Dreamworks, PG-13)
  Tom Selleck, Kate Capshaw, and Ellen Degeneres star in this charming film about a New England town turned upside down by an unsigned love letter.
- Almost any film based on a Nicholas Sparks novel
  Someone finds a letter that changes everything. Lessons are learned. Hearts are broken and mended.

February

In February we celebrate love and African American History Month. What better time to feature some African-American romance?

- *Preacher's Wife* (1996; Touchstone, PG)
  Starring Whitney Houston, Courtney B. Vance and Denzel Washington in this charming remake of the classic film *The Bishop's Wife*. An overworked preacher prays for help to save his congregation. Instead he gets Dudley, an angel determined to help save his marriage.
- *Love & Basketball* (2000; New Line Cinema, PG-13)
  Omar Epps and Sanaa Lathan star as Quincy and Monica, who bond as kids over a shared passion for basketball. Their relationship evolves as they become adults and struggle to balance their romance with their dreams of basketball careers.
- *Why Did I Get Married?* (2007; Lion's Gate, PG-13)
  Tyler Perry directed this film about three couples who vacation together once a year and ask the question, why did I get married? Followed up with *Why Did I Get Married Too?* (2010; Lionsgate, PG-13).
- *Just Wright* (2010; Fox Searchlight, PG)
  Queen Latifa stars as a physical therapist who finds herself falling for her patient, an injured basketball player who seems to be falling for her friend.

March

In honor of St Patrick's Day and Irish American Heritage Month, some films of, about, and featuring Ireland might go over quite nicely.

- *The Quiet Man* (1952; Olive Films, NR)
  The 1952 classic film directed by John Ford stars John Wayne as the titular quiet man, a retired boxer who returns to the Irish town of his youth and falls in love with the not-so-quiet Maureen O'Hara.
- *Into the West* (1992; Echo Bridge, PG)
  A beautiful white stallion appears to a Traveler grandfather and his two grandsons, who take the horse to live with them in their tenement apartment. When the horse is stolen by a corrupt policeman, the children come up with a brave plan to rescue it.

- *Waking Ned Devine* (1998; 20th Century Fox, PG)
  When poor Ned dies from shock after winning the lottery, his friends decide that Ned would want them to enjoy his good fortune and devise ever more complicated schemes to claim the ticket.
- *Once* (2006; 20th Century Fox, R)
  A Czech immigrant and an Irish musician meet on the streets of Dublin and fall in love. Glen Hansard and Marketa Irglova star in this Academy Award–nominated film that has now been transformed into a Broadway hit musical.

April

In addition to being National Poetry Month, April is National Humor Month. This is a great time to screen much beloved comedy classics! There are so many to choose from, but here are some reliable laugh-getters.

- *Bringing Up Baby* (1938; RKO, NR)
  Katharine Hepburn and Cary Grant star in this screwball classic about an eccentric socialite, a frustrated paleontologist, a missing dinosaur bone, a clever dog, and, of course, a missing jaguar.
- *Some Like It Hot* (1959; MGM, NR)
  Billy Wilder directed this rollicking farce about two musicians who witness a mob hit and decide to disguise themselves as members of an all-female band. Complications ensue, one of whom is Marilyn Monroe.
- *Young Frankenstein* (1974; 20th Century Fox, PG)
  Mel Brooks's comedy classic about Dr. Frankenstein's straightlaced grandson who inherits the family castle and finds his disdain for human reanimation tested. But really, it's about the laughs. This same cast making a film about fly-fishing would still have made one of the funniest movies ever.
- *Monty Python and the Holy Grail* (1975; Sony Pictures, PG)
  You could probably do an entire Comedy Month devoted to Monty Python pictures, but many will agree (though some will strongly disagree) that *Holy Grail* is the perfect Python blend of history and the ridiculous.

May

May 4 is Star Wars Day ("May the Fourth Be with You!"), so Star Wars programming can never go amiss in May. Mother's Day also makes its home in May, so perhaps a little Mother Movie programming would not be amiss.

- *Mildred Pierce* (1945; Warner Bros., NR)
  Joan Crawford won an Academy Award for her role in this noir thriller as a hardworking single mother who would do anything for the happiness of her spoiled daughter.
- *Terms of Endearment* (1983; Paramount, PG)
  Shirley MacLaine, Debra Winger, and Jack Nicholson star in this tearjerker about a combative but loving mother and daughter.
- *The Incredibles* (2004; Disney, PG)
  This Pixar film about a superhero family stuck in witness protection features one of the most entertaining and loveable moms on film. Helen Parr, aka Elastigirl, a woman trying to juggle some exceptional children and a bored husband, is sharp, funny and ultimately perhaps the only one that that can save the day.
- *Mamma Mia!* (2008; Universal, PG-13)
  Meryl Streep stars in this quirky musical about mothers, daughters, and ABBA music. A 20-year-old woman about to be married invites to her wedding three of her mother's former suitors, one of whom she is convinced must be her father. Much singing and dancing ensues!
- Of course not all Moms are awesome. Depending on your mood and that of your patrons, you could always consider featuring some Horrible Mom Movies! *Mommie Dearest, Carrie, The Manchurian Candidate, Serial Mom,* and *Throw Momma from the Train* all feature moms that will make you desperately glad for your own.

June

June is Gay Pride Month, and there's never been a better time to find great films celebrating the LGBT experience and history.

- *Longtime Companion* (1990; MGM, R)
  One of the first mainstream films to deal directly with the AIDS epidemic and the human cost of the disease.

- *Beautiful Thing* (1995; Columbia TriStar, R)
  Two teen boys in a London public housing project gradually come to realize they love each other and find solace from the chaos around them in their affection for one another.
- *Big Eden* (2000; Wolfe Video, PG-13)
  A romantic comedy about Henry, a successful artist who returns to his small Montana hometown to take care of his ailing grandfather. Once the matchmaking busybodies in town figure out Henry is not attracted to women, they do their best to find him a good man.
- *Milk* (2008; Focus, R)
  Sean Penn won an Academy Award for his portrayal of the first openly gay man elected to public office in the United States.

July

July is a great time to celebrate the USA with great patriotic films such as *1776*, *Mr. Smith Goes to Washington*, and *Yankee Doodle Dandy*, but did you know that July 2 is World UFO Day? There are so many films about aliens among us. Some of them are even sort of patriotic!

- *Close Encounters of the Third Kind* (1977; Sony Pictures, PG)
  Spielberg's homage to the creepy, scary, and exhilarating alien films of his childhood is creepy, scary, and exhilarating.
- *The Last Starfighter* (1984; Universal, PG)
  Oh sure, they say all that time spent video gaming is a waste of time, but what if all those video games were really planted by aliens to find the best fighter pilots in the galaxy? This entirely plausible scenario is explored in this very fun film.
- *Independence Day* (1996; 20th Century Fox, PG-13)
  President Bill Pullman gives one of the great cinematic inspirational speeches as the world gears up to kick some aliens back to where they came from.
- *Galaxy Quest* (1999; Paramount, PG)
  The fading stars of a cult–science fiction TV show (think *Star Trek*) find themselves kidnapped by actual aliens who want their help fighting a terrible evil. This film is a comedy gem and a genial homage to Trekkies and Trekkers everywhere.

August

Between National Golf Month and National Watermelon Day, August is a challenging month for calendar themes. It is, however, a good time for summer reading–themed films (great films based on great stories) and also back-to-school time. Here are some great school-inspired films.

- *Grease* (1978; Paramount, PG)
  It's the 1950s according to the 1970s as Olivia Newton John and John Travolta sing and dance their way through the trials and tribulations of high school.
- *Ferris Bueller's Day Off* (1986; Paramount, PG-13)
  Ferris Bueller just wants to take the day off, although his parents, sister, and the school principal have other ideas.
- *School of Rock* (2003; Paramount, PG-13)
  Jack Black stars as an out-of-work rock god who finagles a job as a substitute teacher and proceeds to transform his class of fifth graders into a first-class rock 'n' roll band.
- *Napoleon Dynamite* (2004; 20th Century Fox, PG)
  Jon Heder stars as Napoleon Dynamite, the nerd that other nerds hate, who dreams of owning a liger and helping his friend Pedro win the election for student body president.

September

September is Classical Music Month, which is a much more fruitful film topic than Blueberry Popsicle Month, which September is as well.

- *Amadeus* (1984; Warner Home Video, R)
  Miloš Forman directed this cinematic tour de force about the life of Wolfgang Amadeus Mozart as seen through the eyes of his greatest competitor, Antonio Salieri.
- *The Red Violin* (1998; Lionsgate, R)
  The story of a beautiful red violin as it travels through history.
- *Beethoven: Eroica* (2005; Naxos, NR)
  A dramatization of the story of Beethoven's third symphony, originally known as Bonaparte, after the man Beethoven considered to be

the savior of Europe, but eventually renamed *Eroica* when Beethoven finds his faith in Bonaparte destroyed.

- *Mozart's Sister* (2010; Music Box Films, NR)
  An imagined history of the life of Maria Anna Mozart, a talented musician who must watch her own musical career slowly become limited by the strictures of the time and eclipsed by her talented brother.

October

Halloween provides a perfect opportunity to explore some of the classic films of the Horror genre.

- *Phantom of the Opera* (1925; Image Entertainment, NR)
  The silent-film adaptation of the worldwide phenomenon *Phantom of the Opera* stars Lon Chaney as the tortured phantom haunting a Paris opera house. Although silent films can seem quaint and campy, modern audiences will be impressed to see many familiar images that modern adaptations have borrowed directly from this original.
- *Dracula* (1931; Universal, NR)
  Bram Stoker may have published *Dracula* in 1897, but the 1931 film starring Béla Lugosi cemented the image of the suave, charismatic, and deadly count into the public consciousness. No *Blade*, no *Buffy*, no *Twilight* exists without this creepy original!
- *The Thing from Another World* (1951; Turner Home Entertainment, NR)
  This classic about Arctic researchers uncovering a frozen alien led to John Carpenter's *The Thing* and yet another *The Thing* in 2012. Directed by legendary film director Howard Hawks, this *Thing* is surprisingly great.
- *Psycho* (1960; Universal, NR)
  The studios were so wary of Hitchcock's determination to film the story of a loose woman who runs off with $40,000 of her employer's money and finds her way to the Bates Motel. Hitchcock had to finance it himself, and invented the modern horror movie in the process.

November

November is National Novel Writing Month and November 2 is National Book Lovers Day, which provides an excellent opportunity to do some book/film pairings. But November is also Aviation History Month, and cinematic history is full of an amazing amount of aviation history.

- *Only Angels Have Wings* (1939; Columbia TriStar, NR)
  Cary Grant and Jean Arthur star in this romantic adventure about the pilots of a South American air freight company who face danger every time they fly. The romance is entertaining but mostly takes a backseat to the suspenseful flight scenes.
- *The Spirit of St. Louis* (1957; Warner Home Video, NR)
  Billy Wilder directed James Stewart in this biopic about the life of Charles Lindbergh, who tried to finance and build the airplane that would cross the Atlantic.
- *Top Gun* (1986; Paramount, PG)
  The film that catapulted Tom Cruise to the stratosphere and, according to Navy sources, increased recruitment 500 percent.[1]
- *The Aviator* (2004; Warner, PG-13)
  Martin Scorsese directed Leonardo DiCaprio in this ambitious biographical drama of the life of Howard Hughes, a man who was a groundbreaking film director and aviator during the early years of both professions.

December

Christmas and its end-of-the-year trappings clearly dominate the month of December, so pulling out a few Christmas classics such as *It's a Wonderful Life*, *Holiday Inn*, or *Miracle on 34th Street* is certainly a consideration. If you're looking for something more secular for your film programs, there are a few options. December 7 is Pearl Harbor Day, making the way for World War II–themed programs. My eye caught December 5, which is Repeal Day, the date the Twenty-First Amendment ended Prohibition—a very fruitful topic for film programs.

- *The Roaring Twenties* (1939; Warner Home Video, NR)
  Humphrey Bogart and James Cagney star in one of the first films to look at Prohibition closely after its repeal. Cagney and Bogart are

buddies who get drawn into bootlegging after World War I, and enjoy the riches and rags that follow.

- *Some Like It Hot* (1959; MGM, NR)
  Billy Wilder directed this comedy classic about two musicians who, after unintentionally witnessing the St. Valentine's Day Massacre, disguise themselves as women and go on the road with an all-female band.
- *The Untouchables* (1987; Paramount, R)
  Brian De Palma's classic gangster thriller depicting the battle between the honest Chicago Treasury officer Eliot Ness and the powerful mob king Al Capone.
- *Chicago* (2002; Miramax, PG-13)
  The big-screen adaptation of the Kander and Ebb musical about Roxie Hart and Velma Kelly, two sweet-faced murderesses in the Roaring Twenties who compete over the public's sympathy.

Note

1. David Robb, *Operation Hollywood: How the Pentagon Shapes and Censors the Movies*, New York: Prometheus Books, 2004, 182.

APPENDIX C
Films Inspired by Classic Literature

Jane Austen

***Clueless* (1995; Paramount, PG-13)**

Directed by Amy Heckerling and starring Alicia Silverstone, this was the modern Austen update that inspired the rest. A retelling of *Emma* set in Beverly Hills High School, Cher Horowitz inserts herself into the lives of her friends and family with well-intentioned but disastrous results. A modern classic!

***Bridget Jones's Diary* (2001; Miramax Lionsgate, R)**

Although the film based on the Helen Fielding novel has become a cultural phenomenon in its own right, it is more than a little inspired by Jane.

***Bride & Prejudice* (2004; Miramax Home Entertainment, PG-13)**

Austen gets the Bollywood treatment, recasting the story in modern-day India as Mrs. Bakshi struggles to find husbands for her four eligible daughters. *Bride & Prejudice* stars Naveen Andrews of *Lost* fame and Bollywood superstar Aishwarya Rai.

***Becoming Jane* (2007; Miramax, PG)**

A more fictional than historical account of the young Jane Austen and her first encounter with true love. Starring Anne Hathaway and James MacEvoy, this is a sweetly imagined biography about a woman whose actual past is much more enigmatic.

***The Jane Austen Book Club* (2007; Sony Pictures Home Entertainment, PG-13)**

Based on a book—*The Jane Austen Book Club* by Karen Joy Fowler—this film is about an eclectic group of characters who gather to read the works of Jane Austen and slowly find their lives transforming under her influence.

The Bible

David and Bathsheba (1951; 20th Century Fox, NR)

From the era of Hollywood's great sword-and-sandal epics comes the story of King David's affair with the beautiful Bathsheba, which brings terrible consequences for himself and Israel. Starring Gregory Peck and Susan Hayward.

The Ten Commandments (1957; Paramount, G)

Featuring Charlton Heston's memorable turn as Moses, this film has recently been fully restored in honor of its fifty-fifth anniversary.

The Decalogue (1988; Facets, NR)

Famed Polish director Krzysztof Kieślowski created this series of ten short films to examine the Ten Commandments and the complexities of living a moral life in modern society.

The Prince of Egypt (1998; DreamWorks, PG)

Animated telling of the story of Moses featuring the voices of Sandra Bullock, Ralph Fiennes, and Val Kilmer.

Ray Bradbury

Fahrenheit 451 (1966; Universal, NR)

Julie Christie and Oskar Werner star in the dystopian tale of a future where books are banned and firemen have the coveted job of burning them.

The Martian Chronicles (1980; MGM, NR)

Although Bradbury found this TV miniseries based on his best-selling story collection boring, the series starring Rock Hudson and Bernadette Peters was a huge hit.

Something Wicked This Way Comes (1983; Aberle Media, PG)

Bradbury penned both the novel and the screenplay for this spooky tale of an evil circus that lures people to their doom. Starring Jonathan Pryce, Jason Robards, Pam Grier, and Diane Ladd.

The Sound of Thunder (2004; Warner Home Video, PG-13)

Based on a Bradbury short story. Time travelers accidentally set in motion a chain of events that could destroy humanity. Although Bradbury is not credited for it, the film The Butterfly Effect (2004; Infinifilm, R) is based on a similar premise.

Chrysalis (2008; E1 Entertainment, PG-13)

Based on a Bradbury short story. After World War III, a group of scientists struggle to keep plants alive in an underground bunker. When one of the scientists begins to change, panic ensues. Is he evolving, or has human life reached the end?

The Brontës

Wuthering Heights (1939; Warner Bros., NR)

Many a great thespian has chewed his way through the role of Emily Brontë's dark and brooding Heathcliff, but who better to start with than the original master thespian, Laurence Olivier? Directed by William Wyler and also starring Merle Oberon and David Niven, this version is the very definition of a classic. *Wuthering Heights* has also been visited by Ian McShane in 1967 (BBC, NR), Juliet Binoche and Ralph Fiennes in 1992 (Paramount, PG), BBC/Masterpiece Theatre on more than one occasion (WGBH, NR), and of course MTV in 2003 (Paramount, PG-13). Oscilloscope Pictures produced a version in 2011, recently released on DVD, directed by Andrea Arnold, starring Kaya Scodelario and James Howson (Oscilloscope, NR).

The Tenant of Wildfell Hall (1996; BBC, NR)

Though she is too often forgotten, Anne Brontë created her own gothic romance, the tale of a widow who must deal with malicious town gossip when she moves to a remote Yorkshire village. Starring Toby Stephens and Tara Fitzgerald.

The Wide Sargasso Sea (2006; Acorn Media, NR)

Based on the novel by Jean Rhys, this is a compelling reenvisioning of the Jane Eyre story, told from the point of view of the first Mrs. Rochester, the tragic madwoman in the attic in *Jane Eyre*. A young female landowner in Jamaica is convinced to marry a visiting Englishman to avoid losing her land to meddling relatives. But what begins as a passionate marriage begins to unravel in the face of her husband's judgmental reserve and the malicious gossip of her relatives.

Jane Eyre (2011; Universal, PG-13)

Charlotte Brontë's *Jane Eyre* has also been adapted a multitude of times, most recently for the big screen featuring Michael Fassbender and Mia

Wasikowska as the star-crossed Jane Eyre and Mr. Rochester. Other adaptations include the classic 1944 version, starring Orson Welles and Joan Fontaine (20th Century Fox, NR); the 1971 version, starring George C. Scott and Susannah York (VCI Entertainment, NR); the 1980 Timothy Dalton version (Warner Home Video, NR); the 1996 Franco Zeffirelli version, starring William Hurt and Anna Paquin (Miramax, PG); the 1997 Ciaran Hands and Samantha Morton version (A&E Home Video, NR); and the 2006 Toby Stephens version (WGBH, NR). Yes, I have seen all of them, and yes, I fully own that I may have a Jane Eyre addiction.

Willa Cather

Paul's Case (1980; Monterey Video)

Eric Roberts stars in the story of a working-class boy who dreams of joining the world of the rich and beautiful.

O Pioneers! (1992; Hallmark Hall of Fame, PG)

Jessica Lange stars in this made-for-TV adaptation of Cather's story of Swedish immigrants struggling to maintain a farm in turn-of-the-twentieth-century Nebraska.

Miguel de Cervantes

Orson Welles's *Don Quixote*—(Image Entertainment)

Welles began working on this adaptation of Don Quixote in the 1950s as a project for CBS television but quickly expanded his concept of the project. Production was halted upon the death of the lead actor Francisco Reiguera in 1969, but Welles continued to futz with it until his own death in 1985. A version of the film was released to largely negative reviews in 1992 based on a reedit of Welles's footage by Spanish director Jesus Franco. A DVD of this version was released in 2008. It is fair to say that this version is not the version Welles would have wanted us to see, but as an opportunity to see some of the final work of a legend, it is a valuable viewing experience.

Man of La Mancha (1972; MGM Home Video, PG)

This musical merges the tale of Don Quixote with incidents from the life of Miguel Cervantes. It stars Peter O' Toole and Sophia Loren.

Lost in La Mancha (2003; New Video Group, R)

This documentary reveals in excruciating detail (like watching a car accident in slow motion) director Terry Gilliam's attempt to bring the story of *Don Quixote* to the big screen. Unscheduled desert military maneuvers ruin shots and threaten cast safety, violent thunderstorms destroy sets, and the lead suffers a severe back injury, all while the insurance company gets closer to pulling the plug. This documentary was nominated for dozens of awards. Gilliam's film is still unmade.

Up (2009; Walt Disney Company, PG)

While clearly not a direct adaptation, many sources claim that Disney/Pixar's *Up*, the tale of an old man determined to go on one last great adventure, was inspired by the story of *Don Quixote*.

Raymond Chandler

The Big Sleep (1946; Warner Home Video)

Chandler provided the backdrop story of a PI hired to protect a troubled girl who may be involved in murder, but this adaptation directed by Howard Hawks is all about Humphrey Bogart and Lauren Bacall. Their chemistry ignites the screen and distracts from the film's convoluted plot and code restrictions that made a direct adaptation impossible. In 1978 *The Big Sleep* (Artisan, R) was visited again, this time with Robert Mitchum as Philip Marlowe. Although the 1946 version is classic, the 1978 version is infinitely clearer.

Marlowe (1969; Warner Home Video, PG)

Based on Chandler's novel *The Little Sister*. James Garner takes up the mantle of the famous gumshoe in a story about kidnapping, blackmail, and murder. Garner's relaxed charm is a different take on Philip Marlowe than one usually finds, but it works well. Also starring Bruce Lee, Rita Moreno, and Carol O'Connor.

Agatha Christie

Murder on the Orient Express (1974; Paramount Home Entertainment, PG)

A train full of suspects and a cast full of stars! Hercule Poirot must ferret out a suspect while trapped on a snowbound train with a victim loved by no one. Six Academy Award nominations and one win for Ingrid Bergman.

Agatha Christie's *Death on the Nile* (1978; Lionsgate, PG)

Peter Ustinov plays the famed Belgian detective Hercule Poirot, who must find the murderer of a newlywed heiress on board a luxury cruise. Ustinov revisited the role of Poirot in *Evil under the Sun* (1982; Lions Gate, PG).

Agatha Christie's *The Mirror Crack'd* (1980; Lions Gate, PG)

Hollywood comes to Miss Marple's secluded village to shoot a film, and murder soon follows. Angela Lansbury plays Miss Jane Marple with a who's who of suspects, including Rock Hudson, Elizabeth Taylor, Kim Novak, Tony Curtis, and a very young uncredited Pierce Brosnan.

Joseph Conrad

***The Duellists* (1977; Shout Factory, PG)**

Based on the Joseph Conrad short story *The Duel*, Harvey Keitel and Keith Carradine star as two officers in the French army who allow an unintentional insult transform into years of mutual loathing and multiple duels. This film was Ridley Scott's feature-film directorial debut.

***Apocalypse Now* (1979; Lionsgate, R)**

Francis Ford Coppola's tour de force adaptation of Conrad's novel *Heart of Darkness*. Coppola changed the setting from Colonial Africa to Vietnam during the war, but kept faith with the dark story of lost innocence and madness. Starring Martin Sheen and Marlon Brando.

***Hearts of Darkness: A Filmmaker's Apocalypse* (1991; Paramount, R)**

Documentary about the making of the film *Apocalypse Now*, filmed by director Francis Ford Coppola's wife, Eleanor. While interesting as a historical film document, it is also a fascinating look at how one man's obsession to make a film begins to show bizarre similarities to the subject matter of his film.

James Fenimore Cooper

***The Deerslayer* (1920; Alpha Home Entertainment, NR)**

This silent-film version of the Fenimore classic is a German production featuring a very young Béla Lugosi.

The Last of the Mohicans (1992; 20th Century Fox, R)

There have been several cinematic adaptations of Cooper's famous novel about the French and Indian War, but this version, directed by Michael Mann and starring Daniel Day Lewis, is certainly one of the best.

Daniel Defoe

Mr. Robinson Crusoe (1932; American Pop Classics)

Douglas Fairbanks stars in this unique adaptation of the story of Robinson Crusoe. Instead of being shipwrecked on the island, Fairbanks goes there on a bet; and instead of making friends with the loyal Friday, he instead discovers the lovely damsel Saturday, a lady in distress.

Swiss Family Robinson (1960; Disney, G)

Disney's classic adaptation in which a family trying to sail to New Guinea are trapped on a deserted island. They build an amazing home in a tree, have many adventures, and battle pirates. Starring John Mills and Dorothy McGuire.

Moll Flanders (1996; BFS, NR)

BBC adaptation of the Defoe potboiler about "the wickedest woman in England." Traces the lovely Moll's life of extreme highs and lows, where the law or a handsome man—sometimes one and the same—is never far behind. Stars Alex Kingston.

Cast Away (2000; 20th Century Fox, PG-13)

A very modern take on the shipwrecked man tale, telling the story of a FedEx employee stranded on a deserted island who must transform to survive. Starring Tom Hanks and Helen Hunt.

Charles Dickens

Oliver! (1968; Sony Pictures Home Entertainment, G)

For some of us of a certain age, this film may have been our very first introduction to Charles Dickens. A film classic in its own right, this musical won the Best Picture Oscar in 1969, beating out such wallflowers as *Funny Girl*, *The Lion in Winter*, and Zeffirelli's *Romeo and Juliet*.

David Copperfield

Two notable Copperfield adaptations are the 1969 BBC version (Miracle Productions) starring Richard Attenborough and Lawrence Olivier and the 1999 BBC adaptation (BBC Worldwide) starring Maggie Smith and a pre–Harry Potter Daniel Radcliffe.

A Christmas Carol

Scrooge (1970; Paramount PG)

Albert Finney and Alec Guiness star in a musical version of the Christmas classic.

A Christmas Carol (1984; 20th Century Fox, PG)

George C. Scott is Ebenezer Scrooge in this very Victorian adaptation.

Scrooged (1988; Paramount, PG-13)

In this updated version, Bill Murray stars as an angry television producer who makes the lives of those around him miserable until the ghosts start arriving.

The Muppet Christmas Carol (1992; Walt Disney Home Entertainment G)

Because any story ever told, no matter how great, is told better with Muppets.

Great Expectations (1998; 20th Century Fox, R)

Directed by the brilliant Mexican director Alfonso Cuarón, the film updates the story to modern day to tell the tale of Finn, a poor struggling painter desperately in love with the icy Estella. The wonderful Anne Bancroft plays the manipulative Ms. Dinsmore (aka Miss Havisham) with scene-eating relish.

Nicholas Nickleby (2003; MGM Home Entertainment, PG)

It's rare and fine to discover a feature-length adaptation of most Dickens tales, as opposed to a six-hour miniseries. This adaptation by Douglas McGrath, who directed the 1996 film adaptation of *Emma*, tells Mr. Nickleby's story in entertaining if somewhat expurgated fashion.

Sir Arthur Conan Doyle

The Lost World (1960; 20th Century Fox, NR)

An eccentric scientist leads an expedition into the Amazon to find a mysterious valley where dinosaurs still roam the earth. Remade many times, including a 2011 adaptation starring John Rhys-Davies and a 1999 television series.

Sherlock Holmes

There have been over forty cinematic adaptations of the great detective on film and television including the following.

Sherlock Holmes (1922; Kino, NR)

A silent-film adaptation of the suave detective starring John Barrymore.

The Adventures of Sherlock Holmes (1939; MPI Home Video, NR)

Basil Rathbone quickly became known as the gold standard of Sherlock Holmes and created many of the mannerisms we have come to expect from our Sherlocks. Rathbone starred in fourteen film adaptations in all, in addition to having his voice dubbed into the 1986 Disney film *The Great Mouse Detective*.

Murder by Decree (1979; Lions Gate, PG)

Christopher Plummer steps into the role, this time chasing Jack the Ripper.

The Hound of the Baskervilles (1988; MPI Home Video, NR)

Despite many adaptations in the intervening years, it was Jeremy Brett who lifted the mantle of "the" Sherlock Holmes from Basil Rathbone's shoulders in the 1980s for the BBC series.

Young Sherlock Holmes (1988; Paramount, PG-13)

Steven Spielberg and Barry Levinson teamed up to produce this clever story of the adolescent Sherlock's adventures solving a series of bizarre suicides.

Sherlock Holmes (2009; Warner Home Video, PG-13) and *Sherlock Holmes: Game of Shadows* (2011; Village Roadshow, PG-13)

Director Guy Ritchie and stars Robert Downey Jr. and Jude Law teamed up to reinvent Sherlock Holmes once again, adding street-brawling skills to the detective's famous intelligence and creating twisty plots with dashes of magic and steampunk.

Sherlock (2009; BBC, NR)

BBC's latest television adaptation casts Sherlock in the modern day as a moody, difficult sociopath who is still as brilliant and entertaining as ever. Starring Benedict Cumberbatch and Martin Freeman.

Alexandre Dumas

The Three Musketeers

A story put to film dozens of times, including a silent version, a Spanish version, a Barbie version, and more than one Asian action-flick version. Some of the more notable versions include the 1921 silent version, starring the swashbuckling Douglas Fairbanks (Kino, NR); the 1948 version, which stars Gene Kelly as D'Artagnan (Warner Home Video, NR); and the 1975 version, with Michael York, Oliver Reed and Raquel Welch (Studio Canal, PG).

The Man in the Iron Mask (1939; Hen's Tooth Productions, NR)

Early adaptation of the dramatic tale of the mysterious Man in the Iron Mask. In this version, crazed Louis XIV discovers he has an identical twin who has been raised by the brave musketeer D'Artagnan. Remade several times, including the 1998 version starring Leonardo DiCaprio (MGM, PG-13).

Sneakers (1992; Universal, PG-13)

Although it may seem a stretch, this delightful comic thriller—about a team of hackers hired for a government job that quickly becomes a dangerous game of cat and mouse—shares a beating heart with *The Count of Monte Cristo*. I can't tell you how without giving it away, so read the book and then watch the movie! Starring Robert Redford, River Phoenix, Dan Aykroyd, Sidney Poitier, and a mystery guest to be revealed later.

Queen Margot (1994; Touchstone, R)

French adaptation of the story of a beautiful Catholic princess used as a pawn in an arranged marriage to stop war between Catholics and Protestants. Starring Isabelle Adjani and Daniel Auteuil, the film is bloody, sexy, and brilliant.

George Eliot

Silas Marner (1985; Warner Home Video, NR)

After being falsely accused of theft, Silas Marner lives as a recluse and a miser until chance brings an orphan to his door. Starring Sir Ben Kingsley.

Middlemarch (1994; Warner Home Video, NR)

The impact of the Industrial Revolution on the town of Middlemarch and its inhabitants is portrayed in this miniseries.

Daniel Deronda (2002; BBC, NR)

Gwendolen Harleth is drawn to the intelligent and selfless Daniel Deronda, but her desire for financial security drives her to a marriage of convenience.

E. M. Forster

A Passage to India (1984; Columbia TriStar, PG)

David Lean's Academy Award–winning adaptations of Forster's novel about simmering cultural relations between colonial British and Indians in 1920s India was the great director's last film. Starring Judy Davis, Victor Banerjee, Peggy Ashcroft, and Alec Guinness.

Maurice (1987; Homevision, R)

Forster's painful story of a man struggling with homosexuality and class in repressive Edwardian England was not published until after his death. The producer/director team of Ismail Merchant and James Ivory adapted the story to film. Starring Hugh Grant, Rupert Graves, and James Wilby.

Howard's End (1992; Criterion Collection, PG)

Forster's devastating critique of class and gender struggles in early 1900s England. A wealthy businessman, played by Anthony Hopkins, refuses to honor his dead wife's bequest of her family home to a pair of middle-class sisters. Meanwhile the sisters befriend a working-class family who are devastated by a casual decision made by the wealthy businessman. Produced and directed by the Merchant Ivory team and written by Ruth Prawer Jhabvala; also starring Emma Thompson, Vanessa Redgrave, and Helena Bonham Carter.

Where Angels Fear to Tread (1992; Image Entertainment, PG)

A custody battle ensues when a rich Englishwoman married to a middle-class Italian dies in childbirth. Directed by Charles Sturridge and starring Helena Bonham Carter, Judy Davis, and Rupert Graves.

A Room with a View (2007; WGBH, NR)

Although the Academy Award–winning Merchant Ivory version starring Maggie Smith, Helena Bonham Carter, and Daniel Day Lewis is heartbreakingly out of print as of this writing, there is still a very lovely Masterpiece Theatre version of the story of Lucy Honeychurch, a young woman who finds herself torn between her heart and family obligation during an adventurous visit to Rome.

Greek Mythology

***Orpheus* (1950; The Criterion Collection)**

An update of the myth of Orpheus by master of French cinema Jean Cocteau. A poet dallies with Death until he must enter the underworld to rescue his wife Eurydice.

***Hercules* (1957) and *Hercules Unchained* (1959; Marathon Music & Video)**

Before they turned to the spaghetti western, Italian cinema focused on "sword & sandal" flicks inspired by the Bible and Greek & Roman mythology. *Hercules & Hercules Unchained* starred bodybuilder turned actor Steve Reeves & made him an international superstar. Over twenty *Hercules* films were made during the '50s and '60s, and many went on to be staples of Saturday morning TV in the United States, as well as becoming fodder for *Mystery Science Theater 3000*. It's safe to say that these first two hew the closest to the myths upon which they are based (which is to say not very closely) with later films in the series having Hercules fight zombies and moon men and hang with the Three Stooges.

***Oedipus Rex* (1957; Image Entertainment)**

Directed by Tyrone Guthrie and starring Douglas Campbell, this adaptation of the tragedy by Sophocles is performed by the Stratford Ontario Shakespearean Festival Players in traditional Greek masks.

***Black Orpheus* (1959; The Criterion Collection)**

Made in Brazil by French director Marcel Camus, this take on the myth of Orpheus is set during Carnival in Rio de Janeiro. The film features the music of Antonio Carlos Jobim and Luiz Bonfá. It won the Palm D'Or, the BAFTA, the Golden Globe, and the Academy Award for Best Foreign Language Film. It was remade in 1999 by Brazillian director Carlos Diegues as *Orfeu*.

***Antigone* (1961; Kino Video)**

Based on the play by Sophocles, this Greek adaptation stars Irene Papas as the proud Antigone, who defies the king to give her brother a proper burial. Spoiler alert! In the finest Greek tradition, it doesn't end well.

Electra (1962; MGM, NR), *The Trojan Women* (1971; Kino, NR) and *Iphigenia* (1977; MGM, NR)

Greek director Mihalis Kakogiannis, also famous for the film *Zorba the Greek*, directed this trilogy of Greek tragedies centered around powerful women. Greek actress Irene Papas served as his muse in all three films, portraying Electra, Helen, and Iphigenia. *The Trojan Women* also stars Katherine Hepburn, Vanessa Redgrave, and Geneviève Bujold.

Jason and the Argonauts (1963; Columbia TriStar Home Entertainment)

Based on the myth of Jason and the golden fleece, this film featured groundbreaking stop-motion animation to create the fabulous creatures Jason must battle.

Clash of the Titans (1981; Warner Home Video, PG)

Based on the myth of Perseus, this epic action-and-adventure tale stars Harry Hamlin, Laurence Olivier, Maggie Smith, Ursula Andress, and a cast of thousands. Perseus must battle Medusa and the Kraken to save the lovely Princess Andromeda. It was remade in 2010 with more CGI and less Laurence Olivier (Warner Home Video, PG-13).

Hercules (1997; Walt Disney Pictures, G)

To save Mount Olympus from the evil Hades, Hercules must choose between the love of a lovely young woman or becoming a true hero. Chances are excellent that citizens of ancient Greece and Rome would not recognize this story one bit.

O Brother, Where Art Thou? (2000; Touchstone, PG-13)

The Cohen Brothers' classic retelling of Homer's *Odyssey*, set in the 1930s rural South.

Percy Jackson and the Olympians: The Lightening Thief (2010; 20th Century Fox Home Entertainment, PG)

Based on the delightful novels by Rick Riordin and directed by Chris Columbus, Percy Jackson brings Greek mythology to the modern age. Percy Jackson discovers he is a demigod, one many half-human/half–Greek god children, who must train to fight a long list of evil creatures out to punish the gods or just cause mischief.

Dashiell Hammett

The Thin Man (1934; Warner Home Video, NR)

The first of six films based on the Hammett novel about the witty and urbane Nick and Nora Charles, who solve crimes mostly to alleviate boredom. William Powell and Myrna Loy star as the most delightful couple ever to banter their way through crime.

The Maltese Falcon (1941; Warner Home Video, NR)

Before Humphrey Bogart was Philip Marlowe, he was Sam Spade, the wisecracking detective searching for a missing statue after the death of his partner. Directed by John Huston, this is a tour de force of noir filmmaking.

Yojimbo (1961; Criterion Collection, NR)

Director Akira Kurosawa has credited Hammett's stories, including *The Glass Key*, as inspiration for his classic film about a cunning *rōnin* who pits two gangs against each other to free the town they control. The Coen Brothers also credited the work of Hammett as inspiration for the films *Blood Simple* (1984; MGM, R) and *Miller's Crossing* (1990; 20th Century Fox, R).

Brick (2005; Universal, R)

Brick isn't based on a Dashiell Hammett novel, but this original story written and directed by Rian Johnson is as surely the child of the hard-boiled detective greats like Chandler and Hammett, as blondes are dangerous, brunettes are more dangerous, and the pie at Coffee and Pie, Oh My! is pretty good.

Thomas Hardy

Far from the Madding Crowd (1967; Warner Home Video, NR)

Starring Julie Christie, Peter Finch, and Terence Stamp. A flirtatious, willful young woman inherits a large farm and captures the hearts of three very different men. Also adapted by PBS in 1998.

Tess of the D'Urbervilles (1998; A&E Home Video, NR and 2008; BBC Video, NR)

The tale of Tess Durbeyfield, a poor girl whose family sends her to live with wealthy relations with tragic results.

The Claim (2000; MGM, R)

Fascinating adaptation of *The Mayor of Casterbridge* transplanted to the American West. A prospector sells his wife and daughter to another gold miner for the rights to a mine. Directed by Michael Winterbottom and starring Wes Bentley and Milla Jovovich.

Tamara Drewe (2010; Sony, R)

This clever adaptation of *Far from the Madding Crowd* set in the modern English countryside is based on a graphic novel by Posy Simmonds. Tamara was an ugly duckling when she left many years ago, but now back to her family farm with a fancy job and new nose, she quickly and carelessly devastates the hearts of all the men in town, married and unmarried alike.

Trishna (2011; MPI Home Video, R)

The third of director Michael Winterbottom's Hardy remakes (including *The Claim* and *Jude*, currently out of print) is *Tess of the D'Urbervilles* set in modern India. Starring Freida Pinto and Riz Ahmed.

Nathaniel Hawthorne

The Scarlet Letter (1979; WGBH, NR)

An Emmy Award–winning production of the story of unwed mother Hester Prynne, who is forced to wear a badge of shame while the father of her child suffers no consequences.

Rappacini's Daughter (1980; Monterey Video, NR)

Based on a short story by Hawthorne, this interesting twist on the story of Rapunzel tells the story of a girl made to tend her father's garden of poisonous plants. Although she becomes resistant to their poison, she becomes poisonous to others.

Easy A (2010; Screen Gems, PG-13)

In this lighthearted interpretation of *The Scarlet Letter*, a responsible high school student finds her reputation trashed when, as a favor to a friend, she allows it to be known that she slept with him, even though she did not. Starring Emma Stone, Amanda Bynes, and Thomas Hayden Church.

Henry James

The Heiress (1949; Universal, NR)

Academy Award–winning adaptation of the James novel *Washington Square*. A woman's father threatens to disinherit her if she marries the man she loves. Directed by William Wyler; starring Olivia De Havilland and Montgomery Clift.

The Innocents (1961; 20th Century Fox, NR)

Masterful adaptation of James's gothic horror novel *Turn of the Screw*, about a governess who begins to fear that the children in her care are under threat from ghosts and demonic possession. Directed by Jack Clayton and starring Deborah Kerr, *The Innocents* is one of the best *Turn of the Screw* adaptations. Other adaptations include a 1999 Masterpiece Theatre production (WGBH, NR) and a more "horror" than "suspense" version called *In a Dark Place* (First Look, R) starring Leelee Sobieski. Although not an adaptation of the James story, the 2001 film *The Others* (Dimension, PG-13), directed by Alejandro Amenábar and starring Nicole Kidman, is more than a little influenced by *Turn of the Screw* and *The Innocents*.

The Nightcomers (1972; Lions Gate, R)

If it didn't have Marlon Brando in it, I probably wouldn't include this title on the list, but for the "what the heck" of it, this odd horror movie presents itself as a prequel to *Turn of the Screw*, examining the twisted relationship of the gardener Quint and governess Miss Jessel, who eventually become the objects of such hysteria for the next governess in *The Turn of the Screw*. This literal interpretation of the events preceding the arrival of the governess in *Turn of the Screw* steps on the heart of the suspense of James's work, but, hey, it's Marlon Brando.

The Bostonians (1984; Homevision, NR)

A Merchant Ivory adaptation of the tragicomic tale set in post–Civil War Boston, where a young woman is torn between a charismatic suffragette and her cousin, a conservative Southern lawyer. Starring Christopher Reeve, Vanessa Redgrave, and Jessica Tandy.

Portrait of a Lady (1996; EONE Films, PG-13)

A fiercely independent woman inherits a large amount of money, which brings her to the attention of unscrupulous gold diggers. Directed by Jane Campion and starring Nicole Kidman, Christian Bale, and John Malkovich.

The Golden Bowl (2000; Lions Gate, R)

A Merchant Ivory adaptation of the story of a poor Italian aristocrat who weds the daughter of a wealthy tycoon for her money, despite being in love with her friend.

Patrick O'Brian

Master and Commander (2003; 20th Century Fox, PG-13)

The unlikely friendship of a British Naval captain and his ship's doctor is tested when the ship must leave off exploring to chase an enemy vessel. Starring Russell Crowe and Paul Bettany.

George Orwell

The Mill on the Floss (1978; Warner Home Video, NR)

BBC adaptation of the tale of brother and sister Tom and Maggie Tulliver, whose close relationship is tried by their conflicting personalities.

Animal Farm (1999; Vivendi, PG)

This made-for-TV version of Orwell's satire of Stalinist Russia features special effects work from Jim Henson's Creature Shop and the voice work of Peter Ustinov, Patrick Stewart, Julia Ormond, and Kelsey Grammer.

Edmond Rostand

Cyrano de Bergerac (1950; Olive Films, NR)

José Ferrer won an Academy Award for his famous portrayal of the poet and swordsman with the exceptional nose who woos the woman he loves on behalf of another man. In 2008 Kevin Klein won an Emmy for his portrayal of Cyrano for the PBS Great Performances series, which also starred Jennifer Garner (Image Entertainment, NR).

Roxanne (1987; Columbia Tri-Star, PG)

Steve Martin wrote and starred in this modern update of Cyrano. As a small-town fire chief, C. D. Bales is charming, funny, and beloved by the whole town, but he is not beloved by Roxanne, the woman of his dreams, who only has eyes for one of his hunky firemen, who asks C. D.'s help in wooing the lovely Roxanne. Also starring Daryl Hannah and Shelley Duvall.

The Truth about Cats and Dogs (1996; Anchor Bay, PG-13)

The story of Cyrano flipped on its head. A shy radio–talk show host misrepresents herself to a man she's attracted to and then panics when he asks her out on a date. She convinces her beautiful neighbor to go on the date in her stead, and many complications ensue. Starring Janeane Garofalo, Ben Chaplin, and Uma Thurman.

The Russians

War and Peace (1956; Paramount, NR)

Epic if decidedly expurgated version of Leo Tolstoy's story of Russia during the Napoleonic Wars. Directed by King Vidor and starring Audrey Hepburn, Henry Fonda, and a cast of thousands! Has also been adapted in Russian (1968; Kultur, NR) and as a miniseries (1972; BBC, NR).

The Brothers Karamazov (1958; Warner Home Video, NR)

This version of the tale of battling brothers by Fyodor Dostoevsky stars Yul Brynner and William Shatner, so prepare for lots of dramatic eyebrow work.

Lolita (1962; Warner Home Video, NR)

Stanley Kubrick's adaptation of the scandalous Nabokov novel about a middle-aged man obsessed with a teenage girl. Starring James Mason, Shelley Winters, Sue Lyon, and Peter Sellers.

Doctor Zhivago (1965; Warner Home Video)

David Lean directed this award-winning adaptation of the Boris Pasternak novel about a man whose love for a beautiful woman draws him into the Bolshevik revolution. Starring Omar Sharif, Julie Christie, and Alec Guinness. It was also adapted by the BBC in 2002, starring Keira Knightley and Sam Neill (Acorn Media, NR).

Despair (1978; Olive Films, NR)

Cinematic adaptation of the novel by Vladimir Nabokov about a man who becomes obsessed with a man he insists is his doppelganger.

The Last Station (2009; Sony, R)

Although not adapted from a Russian novel, this film is a fascinating look at the later years of Leo Tolstoy. At the height of his fame and power in Russia and surrounded by sycophants and government agents, Tolstoy declares he will renounce his title, property, and wealth for the good of the Russian people, much to the dismay of his loyal wife of fifty years. Starring Helen Mirren, Christopher Plummer, and James McAvoy.

Crime and Punishment (2011; Ismak, NR)

A Russian adaptation of the Dostoevsky story of a man unable to escape his guilt over a crime committed in desperation. For a more modern take on the issues of guilt, evil, and moral obligation examined so well by Dostoevsky, try *Dexter*, the Showtime series now in its seventh season. The show is directly based on the novels by Jeff Lindsay, but the heart of the show's central question—can a man commit evil for the purpose of good—is all Dostoevsky.

Anna Karenina (2012; Universal, R)

The latest adaptation of the Leo Tolstoy novel of a beautiful woman trapped in a loveless marriage who discovers love and scandal in the arms of a dashing soldier. Starring Keira Knightley, Jude Law and Aaron Taylor-Johnson. Other adaptations include ballet and opera versions, as well as a 1961 BBC adaptation starring Sean Connery and Claire Bloom (BBC, NR); a 1967 Russian adaptation (Kino, NR); and a 2000 Masterpiece Theatre adaptation (WGBH, NR).

Shakespeare

Forbidden Planet (1956; Warner Home Video)

Based on *The Tempest* (really!), Forbidden Planet is a classic of old-school Hollywood science fiction. Starring Leslie Nielson, Walter Pidgeon, and Robbie the Robot, *Forbidden Planet* was the direct inspiration for sci-fi classics such as *Star Trek* and *Doctor Who*.

West Side Story (1961; MGM Home Video) and Romeo + Juliet (1996; 20th Century Fox, PG-13)

New generations continue to put their own spin on Shakespeare's classic tale of forbidden love. Both *West Side Story* and Baz Luhrmann's *Romeo + Juliet* do so with wild abandon and little concern of what the parents of the day might think.

Ran (1985; The Criterion Collection, R)

This masterpiece from Japanese director Akira Kurosawa interweaves Japanese samurai legend with *King Lear*, telling the story of a powerful lord who decides to divide his kingdom among his three sons. In Japanese the character for "Ran" symbolizes chaos and rebellion, which is what tragically follows.

Richard III (1995; MGM Home Video, R)

Starring Ian McKellen and Annette Bening. Recasts the troubled king as a modern fascist dictator.

Hamlet (1996; Warner Home Video, PG-13)

Directed by Kenneth Branagh, this film sets the gloomy Dane's saga in a nineteenth-century milieu.

10 Things I Hate about You **(1999; Touchstone/Disney, PG)**

Starring Heath Ledger. *The Taming of the Shrew* reset in a modern American high school.

Hamlet **(2000; Miramax Lionsgate, R)**

Completely modernizes Hamlet's struggles to protect his dead father's company, Denmark Incorporated, against the machinations of his uncle/stepfather, the company's new CEO. Starring Ethan Hawke.

Scotland, PA **(2001; Sundance Channel Home Entertainment, R)**

Macbeth in 1970s Pennsylvania as Joe McBeth, an unambitious hamburger-stand owner, is driven to success and murder by his scheming wife. Starring Christopher Walken and Maura Tierney.

O **(2001; Echo Bridge Home Entertainment, R)**

Othello set in an American high school. Basketball player Odin James is a school hero and dating the headmaster's daughter Desi, but his uncontrollable jealousy, manipulated by his friend Hugo, will lead to tragedy. Directed by Tim Blake Nelson of *O Brother, Where Art Thou?* fame.

Shakespeare Retold **(2007; BBC Worldwide)**

This BBC project to reimagine Shakespeare classics includes *Macbeth* in a three-star restaurant kitchen, *Much Ado about Nothing* among anchors in a television newsroom, *The Taming of the Shrew* in the arena of modern politics, and *A Midsummer Night's Dream* in a theme park.

The Tempest **(2010; Touchstone Home Entertainment, PG-13)**

Directed by Julie Taymor. Not so much an update (the story is still nominally set in the 1600s) as a reenvisioning, Taymor style, that changes the sex of the protagonist from the male Prospero to the female Prospera, played by Helen Mirren.

George Bernard Shaw

Pygmalion **(1939; Criterion Collection, NR)**

An arrogant linguistics professor bets that he can transform a Cockney flower girl into a lady. Starring Leslie Howard and Wendy Hiller, this is but one of many adaptations of *Pygmalion*, the most famous of which is, of course, *My Fair Lady* (1964; CBS, G). The musical extravaganza, directed by George Cukor and starring Rex Harrison and Audrey Hepburn, won eight Academy Awards.

Saint Joan (1957; Warner Home Video, NR)

Otto Preminger directed this adaptation of the Shaw play about Joan of Arc. Starring Jean Seberg and John Gielgud.

The Millionairess (1972; Warner Home Video, NR)

Comedy about the richest woman in the world and her struggles to find true love. Starring the indomitable Maggie Smith.

Pretty Woman (1990; Touchstone, R) and She's All That (1999; Miramax, PG-13)

Although not direct adaptations of *Pygmalion*, these films represent Hollywood's obsession with the "ugly duckling transformed" plot captured so well by Shaw. In *Pretty Woman*, starring Richard Gere and Julia Roberts, a hooker with a heart of gold is swept off her feet by a rich businessman. In *She's All That*, the most popular boy in school, played by Freddie Prinze Jr., bets a classmate that he can turn the nerdiest girl in school, played by Rachel Leigh Cook, into the prom queen, to which the overwhelmed girl replies, "I feel just like Julia Roberts, except for the whole hooker thing."

George Bernard Shaw on Film (2010; Criterion, NR)

This Criterion Collection DVD set includes three Shaw classics: *Major Barbara* (1941), starring Rex Harrison and Deborah Kerr; *Caesar and Cleopatra* (1945), starring Vivien Leigh and Claude Rains; and *Androcles and the Lion* (1952), starring Alan Young and Jean Simmons.

Jonathan Swift

George Milies: First Wizard of Cinema 1896–1913 (Flicker Alley, PG)

Among the innumerable jewels in this set of the work of film pioneer George Milies is an adaptation of *Gulliver's Travels*.

Max Fleischer's *Gulliver's Travels* (1939; Koch Vision)

This is the second full-length cell-animated feature film (Disney's *Snow White and the Seven Dwarfs* in 1937 was the first), the first to be released by an animation studio other than Disney.

Gulliver's Travels (1995; Hallmark Hall of Fame, NR; 2010; 20th Century Fox, PG)

Hallmark's made-for-television version of the Swift tale features special effects and creatures from Jim Henson Productions. The film stars

Ted Danson, Peter O'Toole, and Omar Sharif. Jack Black stars in a 2010 version, very loosely adapted from the original, which showcases Black's antic humor.

Alice Walker

The Color Purple (1985; Warner Home Video)

It's hard to remember, post *Schindler's List*, that Steven Spielberg was once only known for action films, and that the choice of Spielberg to adapt to screen Alice Walker's Pulitzer Prize–winning novel about the struggles of African American women in 1930s Georgia upset a lot of people. The final result, however, was nominated for eleven Academy Awards and is considered a cinema classic.

Everyday Use (2006, Films for the Humanities & Sciences, NR)

When Dee returns to her rural home from college, she clashes with her sister and mother over some family heirlooms. Dee thinks they should be preserved as folk art. Her sister intends to use them for practical purposes. Poignant and sometimes humorous, this short film examines what it means to truly respect one's heritage.

Edith Wharton

The Age of Innocence (1993; Columbia Tri-Star, PG)

Martin Scorsese directed this award-winning adaptation of the Wharton novel about a staid upper-class lawyer whose life is turned upside down when he falls in love with the unconventional cousin of his wealthy fiancé. Starring Daniel Day Lewis, Michelle Pfeiffer, and Winona Ryder. Also adapted in 1934, starring Irene Dunne and John Boles (Warner Home Video, NR).

Ethan Frome (1993; Miramax, PG)

A man who has spent years dutifully caring for his invalid wife is overcome with passion for his wife's cousin. Starring Liam Neeson and Patricia Arquette.

The Buccaneers (1995; BBC, NR)

Four wealthy American girls in the late 1800s head to Great Britain for the Season in the hopes of finding an eligible nobleman for a husband. Starring Mira Sorvino, Carla Gugino, and Jenny Agutter.

House of Mirth **(2000; Columbia TriStar, PG)**

Gillian Anderson and Eric Stoltz star in this tragic love story set against the backdrop of late-1800s upper-class New York society.

Oscar Wilde

The Picture of Dorian Gray (1945; Warner Home Video)

A man sells his soul in order that a portrait of him will age while he remains eternally youthful. Although he gets his wish, the portrait grows ravaged and hideous, serving as a constant reminder of the toll of years of hedonism and debauchery. Starring George Sanders, Angela Lansbury, Peter Lawford, and Donna Reed.

An Ideal Husband (1999; Miramax, PG-13)

A young politician's career and perfect marriage are threatened by the possible revelation of a past indiscretion. In desperation he turns to his ne'er-do-well friend who may well be the perfect man for the job. Starring Jeremy Northam, Rupert Everett, Julianne Moore, and Cate Blanchett.

The Importance of Being Earnest (2002; Miramax, PG)

Two friends in turn-of-the-last-century England use the same pseudonym, Earnest, to avoid unwanted social obligations, which works swimmingly until they both fall for the same lovely young woman. Starring Colin Firth, Rupert Everett, and Dame Judi Dench. Also excellently adapted in 1952 directed by Anthony Asquith (Criterion Collection, NR).

A Good Woman (2004; Lions Gate, PG)

Based on the play *Lady Windermere's Fan*, a young woman convinced her husband is having an affair commits an indiscretion that threatens to destroy her reputation, yet she is shocked to be rescued by the very woman she believed to be her husband's mistress. Starring Helen Hunt and Scarlett Johansson.

Virginia Woolf

Orlando (1992; Sony Pictures Classics, PG-13)

Androgynous actress Tilda Swinton is perfectly cast as Orlando in Woolf's tale of an English noble who drifts through time and gender.

Mrs. Dalloway (1997; First Look Home Entertainment, PG-13)

Vanessa Redgrave stars in this adaptation of Woolf's tale, which follows the day of Clarissa Dalloway as she sets out to organize a party, and as she reflects on her life.

The Hours (2002; Paramount Home Entertainment, PG-13)

Based on the Michael Cunningham novel that shows the impact of Woolf's novel *Mrs. Dalloway* on three women: a woman organizing a party for her friend who is dying of AIDS, a 1950s housewife trying to organize a birthday party for her husband, and Virginia Woolf, a brilliant writer struggling with depression.

APPENDIX D
Online Resources

This list has been adapted from handouts created by John Fossett and Kati Irons for the conference programs Two Thumbs Up and Classics Re-imagined.

Anime
Anime News Network: www.animenewsnetwork.com
Anime Planet: www.animeplanet.com
Funimation: www.funimation.com

Awards
Academy Awards: www.oscars.org/index.html
Cannes Film Festival: www.festival-cannes.fr/
Directors Guild of America: www.dga.org
Golden Globe/Hollywood Foreign Press: www.goldenglobes.org
Screen Actors Guild: www.sagawards.org

Books to Film
www.mymcpl.org/books-movies-music/based-book
www.oclc.org/research/top1000/film.htm

Box Office
http://boxofficemojo.com
www.the-numbers.com

Film Discussion Group Resources
Movie Forums: www.movieforums.com
Senses of Cinema: http://sensesofcinema.com
SparkNotes: www.sparknotes.com

Film Encyclopedias: Technical, Cast/Crew, Awards, Trivia

All Movie Guide: www.allmovie.com

Internet Movie Database: www.imdb.com

Wikipedia: www.wikipedia.org

Film Reviews

Metacritic: www.metacritic.com

Movie Review Query Engine: www.mrqe.com (Great source for reviews of older movies)

Rotten Tomatoes: www.rottentomatoes.com

Video Librarian: www.videolibrarian.com (Great source for nonfiction video reviews)

Film and Television History

American Film Institute: www.afi.com

American Movie Classics Filmsite: www.filmsite.org

British Film Institute: www.bfi.org.uk

Jeeem's CinePad: http://jeeem.tripod.com/home.html

Library of Congress National Film Registry: www.loc.gov/film/titles.html

Museum of Broadcast Communications: www.museum.tv

Turner Classic Movies: www.tcm.com

Foreign Films

ForeignFilms.com: www.foreignfilms.com (Good resource for the beginner and novice)

Parent Resources and Content Guides

Catholic News Service Media Review Office: www.usccb.org/movies

Commonsense Media: www.commonsensemedia.org

Kids-In-Mind: www.kids-in-mind.com

Screen It: www.screenit.com/index1.html

Parent Previews: www.parentpreviews.com

Release Dates

Video ETA: http://videoeta.com/

APPENDIX E
Template for Film Discussion Group Research

(Adapted from a handout created by John Fossett for the staff at Kitsap Regional Library.)

Title:
Director:
Principal Actors:
Tagline:
Source (if the film is based on source material such as a book or play):
Awards/Nominations:
Production Details:
Box Office:
Trivia:
Themes:
Similar Films:

APPENDIX F
Leading a Film Discussion Group

- Take the time to watch the film (if possible) and do research on the film (necessary) before the discussion.
- Before the movie starts, announce that there will be a discussion afterward for those who wish to stay.
- As the film is screening, take notes of anything interesting that pops up at you, particularly things that relate to themes.
- Offer attendees a handout or bookmark with future film screenings and discussions.

You can use your research in a variety of ways to help you guide a film discussion. Here are some suggestions:

1. Before the film starts, you can share production details and trivia about the film with the audience. If you would rather wait, you can share the production details and trivia at the start of the discussion. Or you can split, sharing some at the beginning of the show and some at the start of the discussion. Trivia gives the audience an easy, entertaining access point to the film.
2. If you use the discussion template (appendix E), consider making copies of it to pass out to attendees before the screening.
3. Start the discussion by asking the group what they thought of the film. Did they like it or not like it? Encourage them to expand.
4. Use information gathered for the discussion template, such as themes, and your notes to help prompt discussion. Themes are intended as starting off points, not tests!
5. As a discussion leader, your main role is to keep conversation moving, making sure no one person is dominating the conversation and that everyone who wants to participate does participate.

BIBLIOGRAPHY

"Advertising Guidelines." Movie Licensing USA: Public Libraries. http://library.movlic.com/guidelines.

"AFI's 100 Years . . . 100 Laughs." AFI.com. June 14, 2000. www.afi.com/100Years/laughs.aspx.

American Academy of Pediatrics, Committee on Public Education. "Recommendation on Media Education." *Pediatrics: Official Journal of the American Academy of Pediatrics* 104, no. 2 (August 1, 1999): 341–343. http://pediatrics.aappublications.org/content/104/2/341.full.

The Bad News Bears, directed by Michael Ritchie (1976; Los Angeles: DVD Paramount Home Entertainment, 2002), DVD.

"BFI List of the 50 Films You Should See by the Age of 14." *Wikipedia.* Accessed January 7, 2013. http://en.wikipedia.org/wiki/BFI_list_of_the_50_films_you_should_see_by_the_age_of_14.

Block, Alex Ben. "Movie Ticket Prices Reach All-Time High in Q2 of 2012." *Hollywood Reporter.* August 3, 2012. www.hollywoodreporter.com/news/movie-ticket-prices-high-all-358247.

Boyse, Kyla. "Television and Children: Does TV Affect Children's Brain Development?" University of Michigan Health System. Last updated August 2010. www.med.umich.edu/yourchild/topics/tv.htm#brain.

Carnoy, David, and David Katzmaier. "LED TVs: 10 Things You Need to Know." *CNet.* June 4, 2010. http://reviews.cnet.com/led-tvs-review-10-things-you-need-to-know.

Denby, David. *Do The Movies Have a Future?* New York: Simon & Schuster, 2012.

Donnell, Wendy Sheehan, and Will Greenwald. "How to Buy an HDTV." December 4, 2013. PCMag.com. www.pcmag.com/article2/0,2817,2344237,00.asp.

Ebert, Roger. *The Great Movies.* New York: Broadway Books, 2002.

———. *The Great Movies II.* New York: Broadway Books, 2005.

———. *I Hated, Hated, Hated This Movie*. Kansas City: Andrews McMeel, 2000.

———. *A Horrible Experience of Unbearable Length*. Kansas City: Andrews McMeel, 2012.

"Fabulous Films." Young Adult Library Services Association (YALSA). Accessed January 19, 2012. www.ala.org/yalsa/fabulous-films.

"Film Ratings." The Classification & Rating Administration (CARA). Accessed January 18, 2013. www.filmratings.com/filmRatings_Cara/#/ratings.

"Fundraising Ideas for Your Film Program." Movie Licensing USA Public Libraries. Accessed January 18, 2013. www.movlic.com/library/index .html.

Greenwald, Will. "LED vs. Plasma: Which HDTV Type is Best?" PCMag.com. December 4, 2013. www.pcmag.com/article2/0,2817,2387377,00.asp.

Heron, Robert. "Buying Guide: HDTVs Up Close." PCMag.com. October 30, 2007. www.pcmag.com/article2/0,2817,2209661,00.asp?obref=obnetwork.

Hibbs, Thomas S. "Juvenile List: What Should the Kids Be Watching?" *National Review Online*. December 29, 2005. www.nationalreview.com/articles/216373/juvenile-list-thomas-s-hibbs.

Hoffman, Tony. "Top 10 Best Projectors." PCMag.com. May 23, 2012. www.pcmag.com/article2/0,2817,2374594,00.asp.

Holiday Insights (website). Premier Star Company. Accessed January 19, 2012. www.holidayinsights.com.

Internet Movie Database (IMDB). www.imdb.com.

Juedes, Donald. "Film and Media Studies: Distributors Whose Films Are Purchased with PPR." Johns Hopkins University. Last updated 2010. http://guides.library.jhu.edu/content.php?pid=22245&sid=159097.

Kael, Pauline. *The Age of Movies: Selected Writings of Pauline Kael*. New York: Library of America, 2011.

———. *For Keeps: 30 Years at the Movies*. New York: Dutton, 1994.

———. *I Lost It at the Movies*. Boston: Little, Brown, 1965.

———. *Kiss Kiss Bang Bang*. Toronto: Bantam, 1968.

Kawano, Kelley. "Teen Beat! 8 Teen Film Versions of Classic Literature." *Word & Film*. August 28, 2012. www.wordandfilm.com/2012/08/teen -beat-8-teen-film-versions-of-classic-literature.

Katsoulis, Melissa. "25 Best Book to Film Adaptations." *Telegraph*. September 10, 2009. www.telegraph.co.uk/culture/books/books-life/6166774/25-best-book-to-film-adaptations.html.

Lane, Anthony. *Nobody's Perfect: Writings from the New Yorker*. New York: Alfred A. Knopf, 2002.

Lee, Sander. "Scapegoating, the Holocaust and McCarthyism in Billy Wilder's *Stalag 17*." *Senses of Cinema*. April 4, 2000. http://sensesofcinema.com/2000/feature-articles/stalag.

Maltin, Leonard. *Leonard Maltin's 151 Best Movies You've Never Seen*. New York: HarperStudio, 2010.

———. *Leonard Maltin's Classic Movie Guide*. New York: Plume, 2005.

———. *The Little Rascals: The Life and Times of* Our Gang. New York: Crown Publishers, 1977.

———. *Of Mice and Magic: A History of American Animated Cartoons*. New York: McGraw-Hill, 1980.

"Marketing Adult Reading Programs to the Public." *Marketing Library Services* 13 (April/May 1999): 4. www.infotoday.com/mls/apr99/story.htm.

McNamara, Carter. "Basic Guide to Program Evaluation (Including Outcomes Evaluation)." Free Management Library. Accessed April 8, 2013. http://managementhelp.org/evaluation/program-evaluation-guide.htm.

"Order Information: Rental." Bullfrog Films. Accessed January 18, 2013. www.bullfrogfilms.com/orderinfo.html#rental.

"Plasma vs. LCD: How to Choose." ConsumerReports.org. December 2008. www.consumerreports.org/cro/electronics-computers/tvs-services/hdtv/tv-types/lcd-and-plasma-tvs/how-to-choose/tvs-how-to-choose.htm

Prigge, Matt. "Six Film Desecrations of Classic Literature." *Philadelphia Weekly*. December 22, 2010. www.philadelphiaweekly.com/screen/the-six-pack/Six-Film-Desecrations-of-Classic-Literature.html.

Professor (user name). "Classic American Literature on Film." Listology. October 30, 2003. www.listology.com/list/classic-american-literature-film.

———. "Classic Literature Adopted for Film or TV." Listology. August 30, 2003. www.listology.com/list/classic-literature-adopted-film-or-tv.

"Public Performance Law." Motion Picture Association of America. Accessed January 18, 2013. www.mpaa.org/contentprotection/public-performance -law.

"Ratings History." Motion Picture Association of America. Accessed January 18, 2013. www.mpaa.org/ratings/ratings-history.

Ravichandran, Padma, and Brandel France de Bravo. "Young Children and Screen Time (Television, DVDs, Computers)." *National Research Center for Women & Families*. June 2010. www.center4research.org/2010/05/ young-children-and-screen-time-television-dvds-computer.

"Remakes that Worked: The 50 Best Movie Do-Overs," *Empire*. Accessed January 18, 2013. www.empireonline.com/features/remakes.

Robb, David. *Operation Hollywood: How the Pentagon Shapes and Censors the Movies*. New York: Prometheus Books, 2004.

Schneider, Steven Jay. *101 Cult Movies You Must See before You Die*. Hauppauge, NY: Barron's, 2010.

———. *1001 Movies You Must See before You Die*. Hauppauge, NY: Barron's, 2003.

———. *501 Movie Directors*. Hauppauge, NY: Barron's, 2007.

Simon, John Ivan. *John Simon on Film: Criticism 1982–2001*. New York: Applause Theatre & Cinema Books, 2005.

Simpson, Carol. "Producers Who Offer Public Performance Rights." Last updated March 14, 2009. www.carolsimpson.com/public_performance _rights.htm.

"Tips for Program Evaluation Forms." Association of College & Research Libraries (ACRL). August 29, 2006. www.ala.org/acrl/aboutacrl/ directoryofleadership/sections/is/iswebsite/about/resources/ tipsprogrameval.

The TV Parental Guidelines (website). Accessed January 18, 2013. www .tvguidelines.org/index.htm.

Watkins, Chris. "Evaluation of Cultural Programs." *Programming Librarian*. Accessed April 24, 2013. www.programminglibrarian.org/library/ planning/evaluation-cultural-programs.html#.UWM-N5Pvuvk.

"What Each Rating Means." Motion Picture Association of America. Accessed January 18, 2013. www.mpaa.org/ratings/what-each-rating-means.

"Who: About Us." The Classification & Rating Administration (CARA). www.filmratings.com/who.html.

INDEX